HEALING TRAUMA
in Children

A practical guide for
foster and kinship carers

Sonia Kennedy

First published 2021 by:
Australian Academic Press Group Pty. Ltd.
Samford Valley QLD, Australia
www.australianacademicpress.com.au

Copyright © Sonia Kennedy 2021.

Copying for educational purposes
The Australian Copyright Act 1968 (Cwlth) (Act) allows a maximum of one chapter or 10%
of this book, whichever is the greater, to be reproduced and/or communicated by any educational institution
for its educational purposes provided that the educational institution (or the body that administers it) has
given a remuneration notice to the Copyright Agency (CA) (www.copyright.com.au) under the Act.

For details of the CA licence for educational institutions contact:
Copyright Agency, Level 12, 66 Goulburn St. Sydney NSW 2000.
E-mail info@copyright.com.au

Production and communication for other purposes
Except as permitted under the Act, for example a fair dealing for the purposes
of study, research, criticism or review, no part of this book may be reproduced,
stored in a retrieval system, or transmitted in any form or by any means electronic,
mechanical, photocopying, recording or otherwise without prior written permission
of the copyright holder.

 A catalogue record for this book is available from the National Library of Australia

Healing Trauma in Children: A Guide for Foster and Kinship Carers

ISBN 9781925644531 (paperback)
ISBN 9781925644548 (ebook)

Disclaimer
Every effort has been made in preparing this work to provide information based on accepted standards
and practice at the time of publication. The publisher and author, however, make no representations or
warranties with respect to the accuracy or completeness of the contents of this book and specifically
disclaim any implied warranties of merchantability or fitness for a particular purpose. It is sold on the
understanding that the publisher is not engaged in rendering professional services and neither the publisher nor the author shall be liable for damages arising herefrom. If professional advice or other expert
assistance is required, the services of a competent professional should be sought.

Publisher & Editor: Stephen May
Illustrations: Paul Haber
Cover design: Luke Harris, Working Type Studio
Typesetting: Australian Academic Press
Printing: Lightning Source

Contents

Acknowledgments v
About the Author vii
What this book is about ix

SECTION 1   Background Briefing

Chapter 1 — An introduction to trauma 3
    Types of trauma 5
    How trauma impacts a child's development 6
Chapter 2 — A bit about biology 9
    The brain 9
    The central nervous system 11
Chapter 3 — A bit about grief and loss 15
    Grieving for the family 15
    The stages of grief 16
    Applying these stages to children 17
    'Tools of the trade' for helping 19

SECTION 2   A Quick Go-to Guide

Chapter 4 — Sleep 27
Chapter 5 — Calm down strategies for emotions 35
    Anger 35
    Anxiety 38
    Withdrawal and Sadness 40
Chapter 6 — Social skills 43
Chapter 7 — Attachment 51
Chapter 8 — Family contact 59
Chapter 9 — Toilet issues (yeek!) 67

Chapter 10 — Eating habits 75
Chapter 11 — Lying and stealing 79
Chapter 12 — Sexualised behaviour 85

SECTION 3   Diving in Deeper

Chapter 13 — Boundaries and routines — longer term strategies 95
    Diet 95
    Hygiene 100
    Sexualised behaviour 105
    Healthy relationships 105
    Consequences and planning for healthy changes 109
Chapter 14 — Self-esteem 115
    Self-esteem development 115
    Identity and culture 122
    Life story work 128

SECTION 4   Looking After Yourself

Chapter 15 — Care for carers 135
    Keeping sane — strategies for self care 135
    Vicarious trauma 140
    A bit about biological children 143

SECTION 5   Further Support

Chapter 16 — Tools of the trade 149
Chapter 17 — Further resources 157
    A bit about eye movement desensitisation and reprocessing (EMDR) 157
    A bit about neurofeedback and biofeedback 158
    Books 158
    Websites 159
    Glossary of Terms 161

Acknowledgments

This book is dedicated to all the devoted child protection workers, counsellors, and support workers who have been not only my trusted colleagues but are still my dearest friends. Thank you for all you have done and the unseen love, care, and respect you have shown the children and families you have worked with over the years.

Thank you to the children, young people, and adult survivors I have worked with and crossed paths with over the years — I hold your stories sacred.

To the two coolest daughters a Mum could ever want — thank you for being so pretty damn amazing, funny, and precious people. I love you the most.

P, you are the most excellent, and G, you are a totally cool guy! I have loved being part of your life since you were little and watching you grow into the grounded young man you have become!

Jody thank you for your encouragement, help and guidance I would not have done this if not for you.

And thanks to all the foster carers who decide to bring a child into your home. I honour your decision, dedication, and your journey.

About the Author

Sonia Kennedy is an Australian clinical social worker with over 20 years of private and public clinical and training experience. She is an accredited mental health clinician and an approved counsellor with Victim Services NSW and has worked with adolescents, children and adults. Sonia has experience in a range of settings, including child protection, corrections, education, and veterans and family counselling. Her professional work experience includes eight years at the Department of Family and Community Services and seventeen years in her own rural-based private practice contracting to a number of government and non-government organisations. She has provided clinical supervision to patient/client care staff and has extensive experience in cancer counselling and support, workplace and relationship issues, traumatic events, grief and loss, sexual assault, and family violence. She has significant experience in treating post-trauma stress reactions, complex PTSD, anxiety and depression. Sonia uses Trauma Informed Therapy, CBT, DBT, EMDR, Systems Theory, Sensorimotor and Cross-Cultural Psychotherapy to help clients gain symptom relief and improve their general life quality. She also has specialised experience in child development, parent/child attachment and the interface of these experiences on adult health and functioning across the lifespan. Sonia's clinical focus is on effective, evidence-based practice in psychotherapy and holistic wellbeing.

Healing Trauma in Children: A Practical Guide for Foster and Kinship Carers

What this book is about

This book is a practical guide for parents, carers or kinship carers to address the behaviour their vulnerable child may be experiencing. As opposed to a text heavy on theory, this guide is designed so that you can access information quickly when you need it for specific situations that arise. Most importantly, this guide offers detailed solutions and strategies for day-to-day emergencies as well as more long-term solutions.

The reality with foster care is that many carers are unprepared for the support and intensive care that these children need. Most children in care do not settle easily, and during their time in care they can become disruptive, which directly affects the foster parents and their family.

Research provides us with the knowledge that children with traumatic and chaotic backgrounds have difficulty regulating their emotions. They lack cortical capacity — which means that their little brains are unable to understand reasoning and find it difficult to change their behaviour to fit into their new life. Sometimes the impact of the trauma on these children means typical parenting strategies do not work, leaving carers unprepared and overwhelmed.

This book aims to help carers understand trauma and its impact on the vulnerable child they are caring for. A carer's role is not just parenting; it is about having the ability to teach children the skills to manage their reactions.

This book is not about medication; it's not about behaviour management plans for children, punishment, judgement, or diagnosis. It is about developing a carer's awareness, kindness, compassion, patience, strength, and education.

Most carers become frustrated as they feel that they take one step forward and a thousand back, and yes, this is normal, but by persisting over time, a child's symptoms will stabilise.

How to use this book

It is difficult to understand how much trauma some children have suffered; it makes caring for them extremely overwhelming and challenging. As parents/carers, we would love to take away the traumatic experiences that these children have lived through — but it is impossible. We cannot ignore the influence of a child's background, and we shouldn't expect a child to ignore their own experience in the hope that it will just go away.

What we need to do is teach the child how to live with their memories and their symptoms — it is their story! We need to help them manage their future, so the past trauma doesn't take over and control their life.

You have opened this book for help and guidance. You will find handy 'go-to' resources with specific information and strategies for parents/carers to support traumatised children to develop their potential. This book is structured so you can find some quick solutions to problems that may have appeared in your child's life. These 'quick or emergency solutions' are found in Section 2 under various topics and flagged with an icon so you can find what you need without reading from cover to cover.

When you get some time (yes, I know….), go back and explore the section dealing with a child's reactions/response; and check out the long-term solutions covered in Section 3 to manage particular behaviours.

You will notice throughout this book some illustrations featuring the 'Trauma Goblin'. He can provide you with a strong visual cue as to what trauma can feel like for children and how its effects can be recognised and lessened. The intention of this character is comical and aims to bring a smile during a pretty intense time.

The most important thing to remember when dealing with traumatised children is to love and accept them just the way they are.

You are the wonderful parent/carer who has made a decision to support and care for this little person; well done!

SECTION 1

Background Briefing

Chapter 1

An introduction to trauma

As a foster or kinship carer you are caring for a child (or children) who has experienced traumatic events at some stage in their life. As an adult we may find it difficult to imagine what a child may have faced and we often lack insight into how children cope with such events. This is especially so when we get caught up with making sure they are safe and that their basic medical, educational and physical needs are met. Sometimes we also have the extra pressure of managing the interactions and appointments with the many individuals, services and agencies involved with the child's care. These multiple considerations leave us with very little time or space to actually understand the impact of the trauma on the child and to gain insight into certain triggers, behaviour and/or emotional reactions the child may display. There is plenty of valuable information and research available about the impact of trauma; by also reflecting on any of our own experiences with trauma (because no one gets out of life trauma free) we can gain some understanding of how it may have affected our own behaviour and mental health.

Many caseworkers, counsellors and support people in a child's life will talk about theories and therapies that can be used to address a child's emotional and behavioural needs. The terms generally referred to include 'a strength-based approach', 'reparative parenting' and 'attachment work', 'trauma-informed' and 'the neurobiology of trauma'. There are many wonderful qualified practitioners that work with children — such as social workers, psychologists, art therapists, play therapists and music therapists — that are qualified in child-specific trauma informed care. If you are seeking a counsellor for your child it is imperative to choose a counsellor who is specifically trained to work with your family in a trauma-informed framework. Another aspect of caring for a child with a background that has included traumatic events is that they will come with a variety of diagnoses, generally several of them. You have probably heard of some of these like ADHD, ODD, reactive attachment disorder, PTSD, sleep disorder and anxiety disorders. While these diagnoses are important they are not the main focus of this book — we are going to focus on practical strategies and ways to help you and the child cope.

These terms are explained in more detail in the glossary section at the back of the book.

Children from traumatic backgrounds are familiar with chaotic environments that are likely to have increased their emotional and physiological anxiety. What we know without doubt is that, first and foremost, children need to know that they are safe in every environment, such as school, at home and social events, and this involves having reasonable and age-appropriate boundaries in place that will provide them with a stable and predictable life. They need opportunities that allow for growth and development; this is our responsibility and part of our role as an adult and as their parental figures. As an example, take a moment to reflect on how you react when you have a bad day: we often get irritable, tired, fed up and want to crawl back into bed and start again. Imagine if every day felt like this. If children are provided with a safe, stable and predictable home then, over time, their anxiety, stress and trauma symptoms will reduce — but it will not happen overnight.

Through research we know that children with traumatic and chaotic backgrounds have difficulty regulating their emotions. They lack what is called 'cortical capacity'. This means that their developing brains are unable to understand reasoning; they do not understand the reason 'why' they need to change their behaviour and have difficulty trying a new way to react to certain situations. At first, parent or carers may have difficulty understanding and knowing what the specific triggers are for these children; sometimes these triggers may remain a mystery forever, however, we certainly know they exist! Sometimes the impact of the trauma on these children contributes to their difficulty in learning from consequences so normal parenting strategies generally do not work.

As adults we need to remember that you can never 'get over' trauma; we can never erase these events from our life, but we can learn to live with them. A very wise trauma worker once said, 'People responding from trauma are having normal reactions to abnormal situations'. As the 'grown-ups' we have a responsibility to help children learn ways to understand and manage their reactions to trauma. We also need to support the development of each child's self-esteem and self-worth, to help them believe they are a good person just the way they are. We can teach children the skills they need to be able to manage their reactions.

This book is not about medication nor behaviour management plans for children; it does not focus on punishment, judgment or diagnosis. This book is about developing OUR awareness, kindness, compassion, patience, strength and education so that we can then help the children in our care. We know that children absorb new skills quicker and easier if the strategies are presented in a fun way so try to use your sense of humour; if you do things together, this will also build the attachment and you will become an ally, a crusader who is on the child's side. Most carers become frustrated when dealing with difficult behaviours as they feel that they take one step forward and a thousand back — this is normal — but please persist because with support and time a child's symptoms will stabilise.

Types of trauma

There are two types of trauma. A traumatic experience can be a one-off specific event — such as being involved in a car accident or a natural disaster — and our reaction to this experience determines its impact on our wellbeing.

The other type is termed a complex trauma and involves exposure to multiple and ongoing traumatic events. Children exposed to long-term abuse — such as emotional abuse, psychological abuse, neglect, physical and sexual abuse and witnessing domestic violence — may develop complex trauma. The long-term exposure to these traumatic events impacts a child's development and creates complex trauma.

Some of the things we know about trauma

Trauma can disrupt a baby or child's secure attachment, it can impact on brain development and can lead to emotional and physical triggers and flashbacks; trauma is held in the body, in the mind and in the emotional development of a child.

Children are affected by trauma in so many ways and the information agencies have about a child's experience can only be what has been reported, what is known. We can never really know the child's entire experience so we should assume that what we do know is just the tip of the iceberg.

How trauma impacts a child's development

There are four main areas of development that can be altered by complex trauma.

1. Physical development

Traumatic events can impair the development of a child's gross motor skills (use of larger body parts such as legs and arms) as well as their fine motor skills, those associated with the use of hands, wrists and toes. Impairment of these areas can make a child appear clumsy and uncoordinated; they may

 Symptoms of Trauma

> Trauma symptoms can be real slippery suckers and they can rear up at any time; even when things settle down the triggers and reactivity can emerge again leaving you exhausted and scratching your head, feeling as if you have achieved nothing. Just remember this is how traumatic symptoms work — they pop up at times and we have to teach the child strategies to put them back in their place again so these symptoms stop impacting on every aspect of a child's life.

> **What is a trigger?**
>
> A trigger is an event (something that can be seen, heard, smelt or felt) that produces an emotional or physical reaction to some sort of traumatic memory. The easy part is defining what a trigger is, the second easy part is recognising when a child has been triggered — their behaviour or reaction may become overwhelming. The hard part is preparing for and preventing triggers — they are slippery suckers. With loads of practice, having some strategies at the ready, and a supportive safe and predictable environment then these triggers will become less intense and less regular.

also have difficulty toileting themselves and maintaining healthy sleep patterns. Some research has suggested that traumatic experiences can lead to disconnection of feeling from the physical body, leading to uncomfortable physical sensations, with pain being felt as headaches, stomach aches and unexplained aches and pains. The high levels of hormones such as adrenaline and cortisol that are produced by the body in response to high levels of fear and anxiety can also affect the immune system. Trauma can also affect the central nervous system, which is responsible for functions of the brain and spinal cord — this is discussed further in Chapter 2.

2. Brain development

You will see a brain diagram in Chapter 2 on page 10 but to explain things very simply, traumatic experiences increase the activity in what is known as the limbic system (the emotional part of the brain) resulting in increased anxiety symptoms and heightened emotional reactivity such as the fight, flight and freeze reactions. Traumatic events can impact on a person's memory, thinking, learning and the ability to manage and maintain physical responses.

3. Emotional development

Because the brain structure is subtly altered after experiencing complex trauma this generally leads to automatic trigger responses or reactions.

When this triggering occurs the emotional response area of the brain (the amygdala, a special part of the limbic system) perceives an incoming threat and the person can become emotionally overwhelmed and goes into survival mode. Children will have significant difficulty understanding how they feel, why they feel it and how they can control their reactions. When our emotional reactions are big our rational brain — the part that allows us to reason, to learn, understand and to think things through — goes 'offline'. This influences functioning and has a later impact on self-worth, self-esteem and developing healthy friendships.

4. Cognitive development (how we think and reason)

As described above, trauma experiences alter brain functioning and increase our emotional reactions such that our rational brain (or the frontal lobe) becomes disorganised. This makes it difficult to learn, concentrate, remember, access memory and develop new skills. Think back on your own experiences of when you heard or saw something that caused you distress and how difficult it was to focus, concentrate or think clearly at that time.

Chapter 2

A bit about biology

The brain

There is so much research about neurobiology and the impact of trauma on the brain that's way too complicated to get into here. In this chapter we'll briefly explore some parts of the brain and the functions they perform to give a bit of the basic biology behind behaviour. If you would like further information check out the reference sources listed at the back of this book.

The *cerebellum* is the bit of the brain at the back of the skull surrounding the top of the brain stem and it is responsible for our movement, our coordination, our gross and fine motor skills. This part develops from birth until around the age of 2 years.

The *brain stem*, also known as the reptilian brain (gross right?) develops from pre-birth until about 3 months of age. The functions of this part include:

- Heart rate
- Breathing

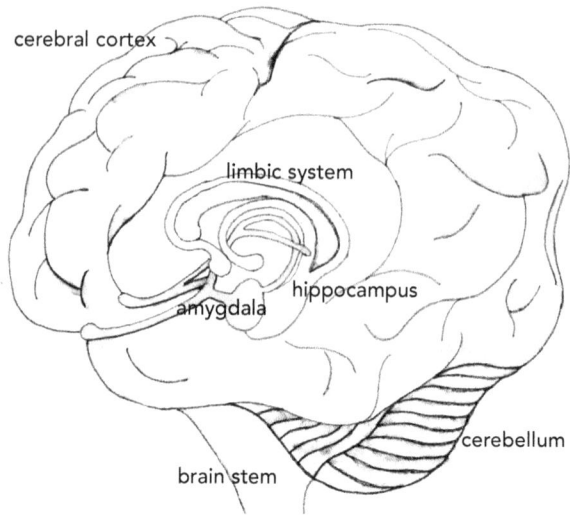

- Blood pressure
- Body temperature.

The *limbic system* — is also known as the mammalian brain. Why? I hear you ask: well, this chunky bit is all about survival and instinct just like an animal's brain. This part of the brain develops from around 1 to 4 years of age. It's also considered by researchers as the emotional centre of the brain.

The *hippocampus* — the hipster's main job is the correct and orderly storage of information into memory in a way that can be recalled appropriately. If it suffers trauma it doesn't work so well — it can end up storing memories incorrectly. This is problematic when there is a 'trigger' that activates a behavioural and emotional response such as when our brain and body react to a perceived threat (remember that definition of a trigger) as if the event is actually happening in the present.

The *amygdala* — this is our 'alarm system'. It's important because it goes off when we are threatened and gets our brain and body into survival mode — the fight/flight reaction. When we have trauma and we begin to think about an event/memory/feeling this bit responds as if there is a real threat even though there is no actual danger.

The *cerebral cortex* — this part is our adult brain, known for thinking, reasoning, being rational, our judgment and self-awareness. It helps us to respond to others appropriately and have conscious decisions around our reactions, responses and behaviours. This part of the brain first develops from around 2–5 years of age but doesn't mature until around the mid 20s.

It's important that all these bits of the brain function as well as they can because they interact in ways that control and direct our behaviour and emotions. Even simple emotional trauma such as a brief scare can disturb these interactions. As an example, remember the TV show and movie *Get Smart* and how at the end of the show Maxwell Smart walks along a corridor and a series of doors slam shut as he passes through. Imagine that he is a trigger that activates a frightened response. In the brain the doors slam closed, shutting off connections between the limbic system and the frontal lobe of the cerebral cortex— that's why it takes some time to think straight after a scare. When you consider that little kids have a cerebral cortex that's still developing it's no wonder they have difficulty regulating emotion.

This shows why it is important for brain development to have a secure and supportive environment from birth to 6 years of age. But luckily we know from awesome research over recent years that our brains are plastic enough to recover and heal from certain types of trauma (neuroplasticity is the correct term). (Phew!)

The central nervous system

The central nervous system consists of the brain and the spinal cord. The autonomic nervous system runs down between the central nervous system and the organs of the body. (Are you yawning yet?) The autonomic nervous system (ANS) consists of two systems (love this word system), the Parasympathetic and the Sympathetic nervous system. Just remember the key word here is *autonomic* (the body and brain do this automatically and unconsciously and you have no say or control over it, and that's a fact).

The sympathetic system is part of the spinal cord that attaches to the organs and when a person is threatened (real or perceived threat) the alarm goes off signalling the emergency response of fight/flight through this system to prepare the body for action.

Like any good story there are always two sides — so the other side of the autonomic nervous system is the parasympathetic system. I like to

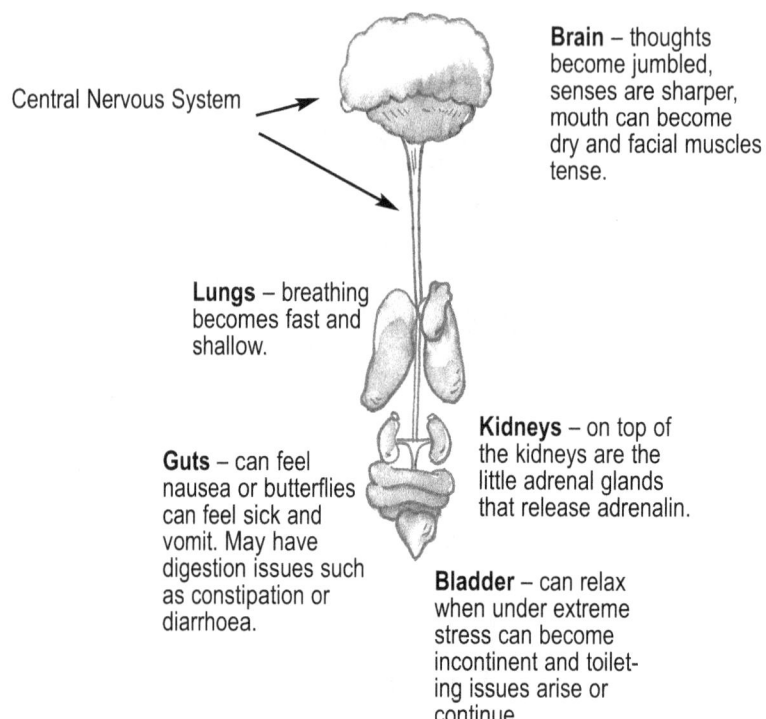

Activation of the sympathetic side of the system triggers nerves attached to the organs from the spine that produce the 'emergency' fight and flight response of the body.

remember this part as the parachute of the body — when released and opened up we quietly and peacefully float down to the ground or in the brain's case — we come back to earth and back 'on line'.

From the brain stem there is this nerve called the vagus nerve that runs down the spinal column touching all the main organs of the body. The role of the vagus nerve is to calm down these organs after a threat is over. When the vagus nerve is activated it stimulates the parasympathetic system which shuts off the fight/flight response. Clear as mud, hey!

In theory, if you are threatened or become fearful your amygdala sounds the alarm that activates the rest of the lovely limbic system, the brain goes into survival mode shutting down the frontal lobe, so no rational thoughts are getting through, and this signals the adrenal grands to send adrenalin through the body to prepare for survival. The sympathetic side of the ANS alerts all the organs to get ready to run like the wind or fight for your life.

Try and recall how your body feels when you have to brake suddenly. Your heart rate speeds up, you may sweat and your thinking brain shuts down, all of this happens automatically — the sympathetic system. When you realise you haven't hit anything and you begin to relax your body may tremble, your hands may shake, you may feel tired or nauseous and your thoughts come back 'on line' — the parasympathetic side.

 A note to remember

> Carers should always remember that the children in their care who have experienced complex trauma have had changes take place in their brain and nervous system to allow them to adapt in some way to this trauma. These children may look like any other child but their brain and body is adapted to threats, fear and survival. Their little body and brain is automatically set and ready for fight or flight — so we need to provide calm, supportive, structured and above all else SAFE environments and experiences to reverse the impact of complex trauma on their system and to allow for the development of appropriate and healthy responses.

Chapter 3

A bit about grief and loss

Most people think that grief and loss are expected reactions when someone close to you dies, perhaps a family member, a friend or even a pet. However, grief and loss also occur when you lose something precious, something you hold dear in your life — this might be a job, a home, a friendship, your health — it can be anything you value. It will involve the same emotional reactions, emotional and behavioural processes that occur when there is a death. Grief and loss can also be experienced when people come to accept that their parents/family members have not been a positive and healthy experience in their own development and life. No family is perfect!

Grieving for the family

Children who have been removed from their birth family experience grief and loss in different ways and they may express this grief as anger and rage or withdrawal and silence, and anywhere in between. A child may have experienced horrific events within their family of origin, however, they will continue to feel a sense of belonging, loyalty and a level of protection towards their family. Even for adults, our birth family/our family of origin becomes our base in life and it feels bad when someone confronts our own dysfunctional interactions or relationships.

As a carer it is very important to never undermine or put down, in even the slightest way, a child's parents or birth family members, no matter what you feel. If you need to blow off steam about their behaviour then do it elsewhere, out of earshot and pay attention to your nonverbal responses (children with traumatic backgrounds are acutely sensitive to nonverbal cues, especially disapproving ones). Children are very clever at separating 'the parent' from 'the parent's behaviour'. Think about your own experience in excusing the 'bad behaviour' of a relative or close friend.

And now for the theory (hang in there!). It is really important to grasp the basics of the theory applicable to trauma and children's responses so you can better understand how your child might be responding or what stage they may be at.

The stages of grief

There are several theories that discuss the grief and loss process with the main one being by psychiatrist Elisabeth Kübler-Ross, who outlines the stages of the grief process. These stages are a guide and recognise that we all may experience grief, and follow the grief and loss process, differently. A person will move from one stage to another in any order and for a varied amount of time, depending on many individual factors and circumstances. The main grieving stages chosen from the theories are as follows:

- **Shock and denial:** The initial reaction is usually described as 'being numb with disbelief'. Shock occurs when a person is overwhelmed; it helps to avoid the pain and acts as a protection. Depending on the person, this may last for a few weeks.

- **Pain:** This is emotional pain that can present as unbearable agony and feels like a person is drowning in a tsunami of confusion. This level of all-encompassing emotional pain can cause physical responses.

- **Guilt, anger and bargaining:** Guilt is felt when a person may blame themselves for not doing or saying enough. Anger can cause a person to blame others for their loss and their new circumstances, while bargaining occurs with a person believing if they do something, behave in a certain way, then what they have lost will be returned to them.

- *Depression, sorrow and loneliness:* Isolation, feelings of loneliness and emptiness may occur and may be accompanied by a deep sense of not belonging. This can be a very difficult stage as a person can lose all sense of who they are and where they fit in life. They will see others getting on with life and feel they are unable to join in day-to-day activities and life in general. People can experience a loss of energy, a disinterest in activities and decreased appetite.

- *Movement:* This is the beginning of adjusting to a new life. Emotional and physical symptoms generally reduce and people may find they feel calmer.

- *Reconstruction and processing:* More adjustment occurs in this stage and people begin to get involved in activities again, thinking becomes a little clearer and they may start to interact socially. They start to develop support and social networks.

- *Acceptance and hope:* This refers to accepting the new situation and, despite the sadness and the anxiety, a person continues to feel they will start to adjust to their new circumstance and begin to feel a sense of self again.

Applying these stages to children

Now imagine applying these stages to a child who has experienced complex trauma and has been removed from their family. A child going through these stages may appear like this and, again, this wouldn't be the same for all children:

- *Shock and denial:* A child may become withdrawn, fearful or appear hostile and anxious, a child may refuse to discuss any of their experience, refuse to believe anything bad has happened and they may experience 'magical thinking', which is an expectation that they will be going home soon.

- *Pain:* Children may experience physical complaints such as stomach aches, headaches, feeling dizzy and unexplained aches and pains. They may have difficulty sleeping as they can experience anxiety, nightmares and flashbacks. Children may have difficulty with their eating and may also have toileting problems.

- ***Guilt, anger and bargaining:*** Children may act out and display behavioural issues, however, the child may have thoughts towards their new carer that 'if they don't like me I will go home'. Anger and guilt are emotions that are very intense for children to tolerate when highly distressed, so they generally become cranky, disruptive and can even be aggressive towards themselves, pets, property and other individuals. Anger can also be a cover for fear and feeling out of control as these children have lost the ability to manage their day-to-day lives.

- ***Depression, sorrow and loneliness:*** If a child has been removed from their family home, they may feel completely confused, fearful and isolate themselves; they may have an enormous sense of not belonging and not fitting in that can increase their feelings of loneliness and sadness. Most people have heard of the 'honeymoon period', when a child arrives and is on their best behaviour. It's generally out of a need to fit in, to be invisible, to be part of something and to be safe. When the child begins to settle the real grief will emerge! Watch out! Most children do not have the words or the insight to explain how they feel and what is happening for them, but their behaviour speaks volumes.

- ***Movement:*** This is when you begin to get a glimpse of the amazing child you have in your care. There are little moments of calm behaviour, small moments when a child makes a new friend at school, begins to show interest in an activity, begins to engage in day-to-day activities at home and at school. Sleep may become easier; eating and toileting issues lessen with support. But don't be lulled into a false sense of security as it won't last and it is not smooth sailing. Throughout the grieving process you will need loads of love, patience, time and understanding to get a little person to this stage.

- ***Reconstruction and processing:*** I would see this stage as the time a child begins to discuss their memories and gain some understanding of their life and experiences, and this may be when you will begin to see triggers and behavioural reactions. Children may start questioning their circumstances as they learn new skills and have new experiences as they are making new connections, new memories and healthy interactions. Children, if encouraged, will begin to seek enjoyment from activities and learn healthy social skills. Support during this process can happen around contact with family members as the child is reminded of their history but they can share and question their memories and past events and remain feeling safe in their new environment.

- *The acceptance stage:* This is the time where the child makes the transition and feels they belong in your family, they have a place, they are important and they fit. This is the time they may rename you or seek ways to become more solid in your family. In my experience, it can take up to two years to reach this acceptance stage and to develop trust and connection.

How can you help?

You may ask (as you shake in your shoes), 'How do I help a child through their grief and loss journey?' The simple answer lies in just being there, being in their space, witnessing their life and their individuality, being non-judgmental, skilling yourself without expecting the child to change, and even though sometimes it is really difficult, do not put their parents down or judge them. Rather, say that sometimes parents just don't have the skills or the tools to take care of their children but that doesn't mean they love their children any less.

Here are a few things that may support the child that has experienced removal from their birth family. While these 'tools of the trade' are offered as suggested strategies, if a child is displaying significant behavioural and emotional responses then please see your GP, paediatrician or counsellor.

Tools of the trade for helping

Feeling safe and wanted

Most importantly, the child needs to feel SAFE and WANTED! Have a good routine and structure, it is imperative for a child with complex trauma to have a predictable environment. You will need to teach the child 'how to be' in your family, what your family rules and roles are, so you need to work out a way to describe these to the child using fun and creative ways. For example, we don't have screen time after dinner because we colour in or play a card game and then read a book, or go for a walk after dinner even if it's only for 10 minutes. Tell them often how much they are wanted in your family and consider how you are to introduce the child to your extended family members and friends. Perhaps ask the child what they prefer, and gently guide them to something that works for you all. Like, 'G'day mate, this is Max, he is living with us at the moment/now. We are so happy that he has come to live with our family. What have you been up to?'.

Hugs, hugs and more hugs

Obviously, you should do this respectfully and at the child's pace. Don't go throwing yourself at them and squeeze them in a gigantic bear hug as this could be overwhelming. Safe physical contact is super-important in developing attachment and safety, and it lessens tension and anxious feelings. Patting or hugging a pet is very therapeutic and will reduce the emotional and physical feelings of stress.

Be curious

Find out about what they did in the home they came from. Even if there wasn't any clear routine, find out what the child liked or enjoyed, such as a certain cereal for breakfast, a certain toy they took to bed, perhaps have a photo of their family in your home. Talk about their parents, as an example, 'What food did Mum like, what colour did she like?', and use this in your day-to-day routine. Make the same breakfast or snack, encourage things they did before to become part of your rituals; if possible and reasonable, then encourage contact with old friends. Ask the child about their thoughts on what has happened and why they are not living with their parent, be curious as to how they see it and compassionate, don't try and change their opinion but instead, at an age-appropriate level, give facts about the events, make sure that you repeat that they are not at fault, they have done nothing wrong.

Create a ritual

Find something they look forward to daily and weekly. A day-to-day ritual could be writing in a journal, having a bath with a chosen bath salt, each night discussing three good things that happened during the day and three not-so-good things, you can use lots of humour with this, kids love words like fart, snot, boogers and spew — make them laugh! A weekly activity could be just going shopping together, Friday night family movie night, getting a milkshake or doughnut, just make it a regular thing (I know, I know, all the sugar stuff, so I am not suggesting this as a given, but try to be creative — if a child collects erasers, stickers, tiny toys, matchbox cars then perhaps get one each week).

Talk about feelings often

Normalise emotions by saying how you feel because every time you do this you are teaching the connection between an event and a feeling and that feelings are okay. You can also talk about how they change during the day, 'I woke up this morning and felt really tired and grumpy but by morning tea I felt happy and had more energy'. This will help children start to notice their own feelings and reactions; even though it is subtle it is important for the child's healing and emotional development. It is absolutely okay to normalise a child's response and to personalise it as children generally lack the words to connect to their feelings. An example of what you could say would be, 'If this were me having to leave my family and live with another family I would be feeling scared, angry, worried, etc., and if I was feeling like this I wouldn't know what to do. Is this how it is for you? As an adult, I know that these feelings will pass and we can find something to do while we are waiting for them to pass'.

Create space

Find somewhere they can retreat to that is warm, protected and safe. Some children will just need to hide out for a while, cubby houses made with blankets and cushions are fun and will also encourage imagination, or another great activity for both genders is getting them outside to build something. A wonderful grandfather built a 'Tardis' with his grandson, it was a great place he could go and hang out, it was his cubby plus it gave him his own space to chill out and helped him socially as his new mates thought it was super cool. Try making a small garden to tend, you can buy little garden containers and seeds or seedlings. This gives ownership, a chore and can bring discussion around lifecycles.

ALWAYS keep in mind that before and after contact with their birth family a child's emotional and behavioural reactions will usually intensify so be ready — more about this in the contact section in Chapter 8.

Sport

Now I know I push this but I really believe in the value of sport, sport and more sport, as well as exercise more generally. There is nothing like a good team sport to develop social skills, gross motor skills and fine motor skills. Social skills include working with and trusting team members and, most importantly, being part of a team can help develop conflict resolution skills and a sense of belonging. In saying this, we must remember that not all kids can manage team sports due to an inability to concentrate, coordination issues and, for some, the noise can be difficult to endure, they may be a little overwhelmed so go slow. There are many sports that are not too noisy such as swimming, yoga, some form of martial art, little athletics — all these will still get the body moving and will give a child a quicker way to feel they belong in a community.

Write a letter

It is best to check with the child's caseworker for information and safety issues on the following. If appropriate, help the child to write letters to their parents (these don't have to be posted). Help them write about their day and how they are feeling — they can keep the letters in a folder and take to contact visits, if appropriate. Set up an email if you can with one or two of their friends from a previous school or an aunt/uncle that would be a healthy connection. Helping a child write to their parent about their day and how they feel gives them a sense of continued attachment.

Visual belonging

Over time put the child's artwork up on the walls and the fridge and gradually display photos around the house of your family that now include the child, as this will give a visual sense of belonging. Children may have difficulty with their identity and sense of belonging, so a storyboard is an excellent way of incorporating a visual representation of who they are. Grab a corkboard and put up words, photos, drawings, bits of material — in fact anything they can relate to who they are, who is in their life and what they have that is positive.

Stay calm, be calm

Don't forget that during this grieving process the child's body is also reacting to the emotions of grief and loss so they will likely be more hyper-aroused (anxious). Working slowly towards helping a child to calm their body and brain will support them developing their normal brain function. There are also many fantastic books available for foster carers to read to children about a child's experience in foster care so they can understand that they are not alone, other children have experienced this and may have some ideas on how to manage. Details are included in the resources section at the end of this book.

SECTION 2

A Quick Go-to Guide

Emergency strategies and tips for a range of common issues.

Chapter 4

Sleep

Children who have experienced complex trauma generally have difficulty sleeping so they need our guidance towards healthy sleep patterns. A child needs enough sleep to allow the brain to process information; this will support their healing process, increase the effectiveness of their immune system, and will increase a sense of safety as they become able to function more effectively.

It is important to set a routine that you can manage, one that fits in with your family, and to be patient in working towards this. Most children up to 12 years of age need around 10 to 12 hours of sleep a night, with a predictable bedtime routine. It's okay to also have some later nights; however, a catch-up may be needed. First set your bedtimes and routine and then we move on to the next hurdle — how to put it into practice.

Most children will be fearful of the dark, they may have nightmares, they may wet the bed. If you have a child that struggles with sleep here are some tips for those nights where they are unsettled. Keep in mind that you also don't want to set up an expectation or habit of making sleep time an active time. Switch things around.

⚠ In an emergency

Your child is running around restlessly in the house (the 'Runner'), or they are lying still in the bed with eyes open in terror (the 'Freezer') or they are unsettled and coming in and out of the room asking questions such as 'how did the earth get made', 'can I have a drink of water' and most importantly 'can we build a Tardis?' (the 'Enquirer').

Here is what you do:

Reset — change the environment

For the Runner:

- Put some music on and have a dance, give them a shower
- Play a quick hand of Uno
- Have a pillow fight
- Go outside with a torch and hunt for possums look at the stars, clouds, shapes the shadows make.

All of these will take up to 20 to 30 minutes.

Target: Discharge the energy.

For the Freezer:

- Get them out of bed, offer a warm shower, warm milk and a piece of toast
- Walk them around the house with you while you potter about tidying up.

Target: Enhance a safe environment.

For the Enquirer:

- Give them a boundary: 'You have 5 more questions to go then it's off to bed, any more come off tomorrow night's allocation'.
- Prior to bed ensure everything is in the room that is needed; for example, water, book, tissue, skateboard, every teddy bear in the house, a trip to Disneyland…hmmmm.

Bribery works really well for the Enquirer so if they go to bed and not come out they can have time reading/looking through a book. Hot water bottles and a weighted blanket can be helpful, as well as a toy or pet to talk to as they go off to sleep.

Target: Reduce anxiety.

Discuss

Talk to them about sleep and what happens at night time for all the people at their school. Tell them they are safe and talk about how the house needs to sleep and may make noises as it is getting comfortable. Acknowledge they may feel that sleep is difficult, validate their emotions and reassure their safety, but also be firm that sleep time is necessary. Tell them you will be pottering around the house and will check on them from time to time.

Calm strategy

- Use oil spray, a meditation CD or classical music, rub their back and talk them through a breathing exercise.

Walk away (for this moment)

Now back away, slowly ... No, don't run!

More solutions for sleep

Make sleep fun by setting up the experience leading up to bedtime with rituals of warm drinks, give the child ownership in choosing which pyjamas they will wear, decorate or set up the room as they want it (things can always be changed later). Talk about what exciting dreams they will have tonight and you will have and can't wait to share in the morning.

- Use a meditation CD.
- Use a night light for a while.
- Use a favourite toy to snuggle up with, this does not mean a child regresses as they will chuck it away when they don't need it anymore.
- Consistently reassure the child that they are safe in this home.
- Distract the child by reading a story.
- Spend some time sitting with your child, pat them on the back, if appropriate, and ask the child if they have any worries that are getting

in the way of sleep? If so, 'how about I take them tonight and I will give them back tomorrow?' For older children use a 'dumping journal' and write them down then take the journal out of the room or put it in a hiding spot.

- A heavy or weighted blanket over the child may promote a sense of safety.

- Create a star chart to encourage rewards for less time out of bed.

- Ask the child what they can see in their bedroom, name 5 things, what can they hear, smell and feel? This encourages mindfulness to bring the child into the here and now.

- Name the things the child may be worried about. For example, 'you have some water next to you, I will be in the kitchen for the next hour, I will leave the toilet light on, the doors are locked and there is a bit of wind around so you may hear the trees outside making tree noises — listen can you hear them? what will you dream about tonight — how about the movie we watched/book we read, who was your favourite character ?'

- Do some breathing exercises together — count your breath in up to 4 and out for 4 then start again (do this for 2 minutes).

- Or breathe in and out in the shape of a box making the box bigger and smoother as you go. Trace the shape of a box with your finger while you breath.

- Use imagination, tell stories that encourage the child to visualise calm colours and calm objects or pictures.

- Spray some oil scent onto their pillow.

- If all else fails — start again! If your child is upside down in bed or climbing the walls and hanging off the bedroom light do some grounding exercises — an easy one is to get them to squat down and tense their legs, arms, ball their hands into fists, clench their jaw and squeeze all their muscles really tight, count to 5 and release, shake it out and do it again — try for three times.

- Massage is known to activate the parasympathetic nervous system which will relax the body. Obviously, you don't want to trigger the

child's traumatic experience so talk it through and try massaging arms, feet, hands or back.

- Colouring in, look at some pictures in a book, for example, dinosaurs, vehicles, horses, dogs, etc. Then try and settle again. Always keep lights low and low music in the background.
- NO screen time for at least 3 hours before bedtime, especially gaming as this will increase brain activity and anxiety.
- Keep calm and stay neutral but caring.
- If sleep becomes an ongoing issue see your paediatrician.

Dealing with nightmares

Trauma therapist, Babette Rothschild, uses a 'dual awareness' to reduce nightmares and flashbacks in adults, it works remarkably well. Using this concept for children would actually prepare them for nightmares or bad dreams in a gentle way and give them a sense of control and power over the bad dreams and nightmares. It's okay to be honest with children in an age-appropriate way and approaching the bad dreams together gives a child a sense of attachment, and being in it together. The section below has been adapted from Babette Rothschild's approach.

Boss those nightmares away

Right, let's boss these nightmares around! Together, draw up a sheet like the one on the page opposite and fill in the blanks (in pencil as they may change). Prior to bedtime, perhaps one morning or afternoon, come up with a title for their bad dreams, like a title of a book, without going into detail of the actual nightmare. It could be 'the yuk stuff', 'the scary dream', 'the bad thing', 'the monster' — whatever works.

The object is to either read this out together or for the child to read it out every night before sleep, reading it word-for-word, encourage the child to see and point out different things in their bedroom. The crucial point is to be consistent and do it every night until the bad dreams go away.

'THE BAD DREAM BOMBER'

When I wake up from my bad dream I will be feeling (name an emotion; e.g., scared)
_____
_____

I will feel in my body (name 3 sensations such as pounding heart, fast breathing, headache, tears in my eyes)
_____
_____

because I have dreamt about '*THE TITLE OF THE DREAM*'
_____.

I will look around my bedroom and know that I am

(their age or the year it is (_____) and I will know that I am safe,

I will see (name 5 things they can see in their room)
_____

So I will know that 'THE TITLE OF THE DREAM'
_____

is not happening now or anymore.

Chapter 5

Calm down strategies for emotions

Here are some strategies you can use to help reduce emotional reactivity. Find what works for your child and have a couple of strategies up your sleeve at all times.

Anger

Anger has a purpose and is generally a protective factor, but underlying anger there is usually fear and grief. Anger can be expressed from big outbursts to lower level moodiness. Over the long term teach a child why they may be angry and the reason behind the anger, such as fear or grief, as this will give context for their feelings. This will encourage the child to recognise situations, triggers and the early warning signs and can then support the development of their control.

With all emotions it is important that you begin talking about and naming feelings as this will develop a language for the child. Name it and describe it. There are many emotion charts you can print off the internet to help.

⚠ In an emergency

- First, make sure you and your child are safe and free from any physical danger.
- Stay with your child but keep your distance.
- Remember, time out is not okay as a child does not have the skills to calm themselves; it is our role to teach these skills.
- Lower your voice and adjust your physical posture to a calm stature.
- Keep speaking to your child with reassurance: 'I understand that you are angry, take some breaths, it's okay, let's go outside and throw a ball or jump on the trampoline'.
- Developing a script will help you stay neutral and calm while you reassure the child — 'I see that you are struggling with your anger and it is my job to help you calm down/stop "the behaviour", I am here to talk and listen when you are ready. This behaviour is not okay and we will discuss it later'.
- Do not ever punish, but use appropriate and immediate consequences when the outburst is over.
- Start yawning and try and encourage your child to yawn, if possible, this can trigger a feeling of calm.
- Play with sand, if you want to be really creative add foam to the sand this may encourage the child to join you.
- Give them a cushion to scream into or hit against.
- Help them sit in the corner of a lounge with their calm box (see Chapter 16) and if needed have cushions around them. This can create a feeling of being safe.
- Use a ball outside to kick or throw. A tennis ball against a shed or back fence is brilliant as it makes a big noise.
- Rip up a newspaper.
- Go for a run outside.

- Put some music on.
- Do tension and relaxation exercises. Progressive muscle and relaxation exercise.

More solutions for anger

- When your child calms, give them a hug (if appropriate) and reassure them that they are safe and all will be okay.
- After the outburst is over have the discussion about what happened, how it wasn't appropriate, what they can do differently next time.
- Keep a daily journal or drawing journal for younger children.
- Teach your child to recognise the feeling of anger in their body and to add a little mantra when they feel this, for example, 'I need to stop, take 3 deep breaths and walk away/draw' or whatever works for this child.
- Develop a 'go-to' box. It might be an old shoe box. Decorate it and keep note pad, paper, pencils, stationary, a book/picture book, stickers, small toys, cards and play dough (sensory things)(see Chapter 16).
- Use items that soothe the child's senses: sight, smell, hear, taste and touch. So music, a soft toy to stroke or play dough, oil burners, a lolly to suck on or a drink, anything to change the senses.
- Teach breathing exercises such as 'smell the flowers and blow out the candles' — breath in slowly to the count of 3 and out fast to the count of 3 trying to extend the number to 5. Teach breathing into the stomach and use their hands on their tummy like they are blowing up a balloon.
- Never punish — did I say this already? But do talk about what is unacceptable and acceptable behaviour and do use appropriate consequences.
- Imagine a safe place. Develop a place that is completely safe where they can go in their imagination this can be something they have experienced or made up. They can take whatever they want into this place, for example, a pet or food. Use this at night before bedtime too as it will help with sleep and to develop the memory of the safe place.

Anxiety

Anxiety may be experienced in many forms such as fears of objects like dogs and being scared of the dark, to panic attacks and overwhelming emotional reactions of anger, crying, running away or withdrawing. More severe anxiety can present as skin-picking, self-harm and physical sensations like tummy aches.

In an emergency

- Breathe it out — use your exercises.
- Use muscle tension and relaxation.
- Try squats and movement — jumping up and down, skipping and dancing.
- Discuss what is happening right now 'I know you are feeling weird, just know you are safe right now, nothing bad is happening right now'.
- Sensory management — name 5 things they can see, hear, smell and touch. Encourage sensory activities.
- If you have a swing or rocking chair then encourage the child to use this to help soothe.
- Distract with activities they can help you with, such as baking a cake, folding tea towels or dusting and sweeping.
- Use a sorting tray and 'go-to' box.
- Use those oil/water ornaments so the child can watch them and then turn them upside down, kinda like a lava lamp (but don't include the strobe and smoke machine).
- Go outside and ask your child to find you three things that are brown (not dog poo), point to three green things, find three flowers. Ask them "What can you smell?".

More solutions for anxiety

- Slowly breathe in to the count of three and out to the count of three. Slowly increasing this to 4 in and 4 out.
- Help your child change their thoughts from negative to helpful ones.
- When they are anxious ground them by helping to develop techniques to bring them into the present — look around, name what you see, say to yourself over and over 'I am safe'.
- Teach the child how 'what you think, makes you feel a certain way, which then makes you do a certain thing'. See this in the toolkit discussion in Chapter 8.
- Imagine standing in a stream and letting all the worries leave your body and float away down the stream.
- Encourage play with, and caring for, pets. Aquariums can be very soothing for children with anxiety.
- Over time you may help your child fight their fear by writing down goals that encourage approaching fears, rather than avoiding them. For example, if the child does not want to attend school then map all the reasons why, set goals for each one and a reward system.
- Get them to imagine having someone by their side, a person, a character from a movie — anything they will feel safe having next to them.
- Use things to distract them, change their environment — go outside, drive to the park, visit a friend.
- Make them laugh. If you are not in a funny mood put on an episode of a comical or slapstick program or anything that is age-appropriate.
- Hug it out.
- Develop and encourage hobbies or activities such as craft, colouring in, knitting, woodwork or anything they like.
- Make them laugh!

- Tell them about your own experiences with anxiety and what helped you out when you were young. This helps to normalise and validate their experience so they feel less different.
- If you can find a group that addresses anxiety in your local area such as the 'Cool Kids' program that was developed by Macquarie University or the 'Take Action' program developed by Griffith University — make the time and attend.

Withdrawal and sadness

The emotional overwhelming nature of grief and loss can be enormous for these children. Some children become very teary, without understanding why they are crying and these feelings may rush out and come out of the blue.

Try using steps the steps below to acknowledge, normalise, validate and witness their emotional distress.

- First, stop and take notice — 'I see that you are teary, that's okay because sometimes it's important to cry, our tears need to come out, how about I sit with you for a while?'

- After the child calms, ask them what they feel in their body. Find out if anything happened that made them sad or did the tears just come on their own. Ask them what they need. If they don't know then maybe say, 'If I were you I would probably feel sad too'.
- Change the environment. Go to a friend's place, walk outside and check out what is happening in the street, even if it is just a quick trip to the shops to grab some milk. Pull out some cookbooks and get them to help choose what to have for dinner or a cake to bake.
- Organise a fun experience.
- Talk to them about what makes them sad and what they like, tell them what you are seeing, for example, 'I notice you look sad and I would like to know what is going on for you'.
- Anchor them in the present, get the child to point to something that is the colour blue, ask them to count how many cups are on the table — use your own imagination, just look around and ask them what is in their environment. Get the child to point, to count, to smell, to hear and to see.
- Distract with activities they enjoy, these may be physical activities or hobbies.
- Use a toy and tell them that 'Jess the Bunny is so sad, how can we cheer her up? Find out what the child's ideas are.
- Play a game.
- Exercise.
- Write or draw in a journal.
- Read a story and take it in turns.
- Nurture and spend time with the child — take time, don't rush or ignore, listen, if they don't want to talk just be in their space until they start to perk up.

Prevention strategies

There are some long-term ways to reduce the intensity, frequency and length of feeling emotionally overwhelmed. Always ask the child what helps them keep calm and try to teach them helpful thinking. People keep on talking about positive thinking, but in cases where children have been abused it can be difficult to encourage positivity. Helpful thinking is a way to encourage different ways of thinking and to create control over thoughts, adding in the emotion that goes with these thoughts can be helpful. This is all about teaching the words that go with the emotion and how thoughts can and do affect how we feel and therefore influence our actions and behaviours.

Approaches that may help include:

- Counselling — make sure you find a counsellor qualified to work with children and be guided by your child's interaction and feedback.
- Teaching strategies, being flexible, spending time with the child and learning about their experience. Be curious and not confronting or judgmental.
- Pets are awesome and are a great way to teach empathy and responsibility.
- Interests and hobbies are important in developing the child's self-esteem and identity.
- Teaching children skills such as cooking, tidying, gardening, even building.
- Use humour and, if you're exhausted, use TV shows.
- Change the environment or view.
- Have a box of picture books in the lounge room or in their bedroom change these weekly and even introduce going to the library to borrow and return books as an activity.

Chapter 6

Social skills

Children who were raised in chaotic and traumatic environments will generally have a low self-esteem and an overall sense of shame, however, they may appear as having a level of bravado, they may be aggressive or shy and withdrawn, anything in between or all of the above. I have noticed that these children generally are attracted to other children that have similar behaviours and may have difficulties understanding and operating within social norms. Children with complex trauma can show symptoms and characteristics of anxiety disorders, ADHD, conduct and oppositional disorder, depression and neurodevelopment disorders such as Autism so you can kinda understand how it might be difficult to make friends.

Social skills are developed by role modelling so you can understand if a child that comes from a domestic violence background may behave in ways that are aggressive and reactive especially when they are overwhelmed. Recess and lunchtime are challenging times as there is little to no structure, the environment is noisy and chaotic so it is understandable that these little people really react like they are unsafe, this experience for most of these children is pretty crap, if you ask me.

How do you change this? Good question. It is important to get on top of this as early as possible because when adolescence hits these issues become more difficult to direct into healthy choices.

The key to supporting a child's social skill development is to understand the reason behind the behaviour. Now this is soooo very important and if you get a handle on this you are more than halfway there and do not ever take the child's behaviour and reactivity personally; this isn't about you, this is about their background rearing its head.

A child won't say to you, 'Hey listen carer I think I am perceiving an incoming threat as I am beginning to feel uncomfortable, my heart is pounding, my head hurts, I want to throw myself under a bus to escape the pressure in my body but instead I will just stand here and hit you in the guts and kick my school bag because at the moment I hate myself'. All you witness is the behaviour.

The one thing that really gets in the way of children having good social interactions and peer relationships is emotional reactivity. So let's get a handle on *affect regulation* and what we can do. *Affect* is the expression of the emotion that can be observed, and as we know, emotions are complex. When one of our emotions is strong, we can control our affect by calming ourselves down on the inside so we can appear to be reasonable on the outside. When a little person is overwhelmed, unable to manage their feelings and is seen to be clearly distressed by their behaviour, this is known as affect *dysregulation*.

Below is a list of emotions to show that emotions range in intensity and are complex. Can you recognise in yourself some of these mixed emotions when you feel hurt? Do you flip into anger, frustration and at the same time experience disappointment and sadness with a little revenge fantasy *(hmmmm,* yes, of course you do!). The difference is you have control. An example of affect regulation may be Monday morning school drop off — you may know an activewear mum looking fresh and fit with a perfect child with perfect hair and matching shoes and backpack and be able to smile at her, compliment her on her latest marathon win whilst at the same time have homicidal thoughts because you haven't slept for a week, you have a cornflake in your eyebrow, your child has just lost their tenth lunch box, shat on your mobile phone and refused to eat anything but chicken nuggets for breakfast! But, of course, you don't yank Ms Activewear's perfect ponytail because you can have these feelings while keeping in control. Your outward appearance and behaviour remains pleasant and civil. It is impor-

EMOTIONS

Calm	Content	Happy	Joy	Excited
Sad	Hurt	Miserable	Depressed	Grief
Guilt	Envy	Disgust	Embarrassed	Shame
Fear	Worried	Anxious	Scared	Terrified
Anger	Irritable	Moody	Frustration	Rage

tant to exert this control because children will learn from your actions and your role modelling and this is significant specifically when the child is beginning to develop their new identity.

When a little person is experiencing affect dysregulation they may become hyperaroused, agitated or aggressive, or they may become under-aroused which will be seen as withdrawn or dissociated. Children's behaviour will reflect their affect dysregulation.

The big one is shame. Shame produces an overwhelm of affect dysregulation and a child with reduced capabilities both cognitively and emotionally, will act out in so many ways such as being angry, sad, disgusted and everything in between. Mostly what is behind it all is shame and fear their behaviour will be varied and in some cases extreme. See how this is not about you but their overwhelming emotional anguish that they don't understand.

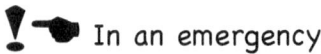 In an emergency

Your goal here is to calm the situation.

- Number one   DON'T TAKE IT PERSONALLY
- Use a distraction technique. This can include having on hand a bottle of water, snacks or things to play with. Those fidget spinners are great or a paper airplane (perhaps leave the nerf gun at home).
- Carry a small iPod with music and headphones, a book or activity.
- Be prepared for transitions — these can be messy.
- One way to connect and calm your child is by touch. This may be holding their hand, a gentle touch on the shoulder.
- If it's safe, bend to their eye level, ask them to find something blue, name 5 things they see, 4 things they hear.
- Carry something nice to smell in their pocket or yours such as a hankie with some scented oil.
- Have a piece of velvet or a big smooth bead they can play with.
- Offer very limited choices to drink such as juice or water.

- A little frozen ice pack in a ziplock bag wrapped in a facecloth to place on their wrists, back of neck or over eyes.
- If you can pop into the toilet and have them put their wrists under cold water or if they can splash water on their face — if this works always carry a dry facecloth.
- Go for a quick walk.
- Teach them to hum or sing a song in their head.

Prevention strategies

- Use role play to develop situations and develop scripts for the child to use such as introducing themselves, how to leave an uncomfortable situation, what topics they can talk about, how to focus on what's around them not listen to what's going on in their head.
- Provide safe, small environments to practice this role playing.
- Teach your child how to give and receive a compliment.
- Explain how sometimes it's okay not to speak and just be quiet.
- Offer simple choices often, would you like milk or juice, vegemite or jam, a shower or a bath, jeans or trackies.
- Always wait until the child is calmer and explain consequences.
- Tell them they can make the choices and teach the child how.
- Have an environment and routine that is predictable as possible.
- How to maintain their privacy. Teach them how to maintain their privacy so they don't have to tell everyone everything about themselves. Most of these children don't have healthy boundaries. Also a script works. 'I am living with my carers because my parents can't look after me at the moment, where do you live?'.
- Learning to read social skills explain how certain emotions can look, for example, happy is a smile, what does confused look like, when you are out for a milkshake make a game of finding happy, confused, angry, frustrated faces, use books or play together.

- Learning how to handle — excitement, disappointment and big feelings. Go back to the affect continuum and even teach them most kids feel these feelings in their body and to notice these and then look around to see if they are safe then it's just a feeling and it will go away even though it's uncomfortable at the moment.

- Teach how to answer the phone then positive praise with something like, 'That's so cool the way you spoke to that annoying telemarketer'!

- Even have a word to their teacher about helping develop positive social interactions.

- Working in teams or just next to others, find a knitting club, an art or craft workshop or drama class.

- Setting consequences on unacceptable behaviour — quick and to repair any relationship or property damage — saying sorry, picking up broken things. Talk about how things made you feel, them feel or even the other person felt scared. Name it. When the child is calm say, 'I want you to say sorry to Alex for hitting him'.

- Remind them the first time is the worst time and, after that, those things get easier.

- Tell the child how you do it — instead of tripping over the activewear mum I say hello instead and give her a compliment.

- Set up expectations — what might happen at this birthday party, what might happen at school, what might happen at the swimming pool.

- How do relationships with peers look, watch movies and comment on how people interact.

- Be prepared — transitions can be messy, for example, lunchtime, moving from primary to high school. Get teachers on board.

- Oppositional behaviour — arm yourself with humour and scripts.

As we have learnt a child's memory is different, learning is difficult and retaining information is difficult. A child's brain is coping with flashbacks, new information is bombarding them all the time and these children are mainly in hypervigilance mode which makes new environments not exciting but scary and threatening rather than exciting. A child's behaviour of managing this may be seen as oppositional behaviour, not doing what is asked of them or refusing to participate. This is awful to witness and manage as a carer but, again, this isn't about you or what you are offering to the child, it is about knowing at this moment they are feeling out of control and unsafe. When this clicks in, my goodness, life becomes so much easier and bearable.

Chapter 7

Attachment

If all goes well while you are growing in your mum's tummy you are born with a brain that is healthy and ready to wire up and fire. When you are born your senses such as seeing, hearing, touching and taste develop. Your movement, both gross and fine motor skills, develop within normal parameters and your breathing and heart rate function in response to healthy norms. The human brain needs this part to go well as this is the foundation for the formation of emotional connection. Emotional connections develop and occur in the early part of life and mainly by attaching to a caregiver. Having a safe and nurturing relationship with a main caregiver is important for a healthy brain. Sadly, this is the period in a child's life where most abuse happens and the worst impact of the abuse occurs, that is, in the pre-verbal stage while all the lovely connections are meant to be forming.

Psychologists Bowlby and Ainsworth (1991) suggest that there a few types of attachment that a child can have with a caregiver. These are briefly described as 'Secure attachment is when the child is nurtured, safe and easily soothed, it happens in predictable environments when the caregiver responds quickly to the child's anguish'.

Insecure attachment is developed depending upon the child's caregiver, the environment and can later be observed by the child's behaviour.

- *Avoidant attachment* — a child with this attachment will display behaviour where they are not very distressed when the caregiver is not present and when the caregiver returns the child largely avoids the caregiver. A typical behaviour of a caregiver that results in this attachment would be one that is angry, dismissive, aggressive and insensitive to the child's needs. The result is a child that keeps at a distance from a person and appears aloof; the child will also avoid comfort and emotional connection as these are felt as dangerous.

- *Anxious or ambivalent attachment* — a child will be extremely upset and distressed when the caregiver removes themselves but will also push the carer away when they return. This is the push/pull type of attachment. Mostly the caregiver is withdrawn, lacks insight and involvement in the child's life and is inconsistent with their caring and unable to adequately respond to the child's needs. The result is the child will act out; their behaviour is disruptive and generally challenging, demanding, and aggressive.

- *Disorganised or disoriented attachment* (this is the worst form of attachment and very, very sad) — mostly this type of attachment occurs in children that have been exposed to ongoing and severe abuse. Caregivers are extreme in their behaviour, random and highly reactive. Mostly these children will be withdrawn and dissociated; they may seek connection with any random person which is dangerous and can shut down and withdraw.

Secure attachment is super important when it comes to identity formation as a child with any of the anxious attachments will have a very low self-esteem, be untrustworthy, frightened, emotionally reactive and have an unhealthy sense of shame.

Then we have Reactive Attachment Disorder (RAD) you will probably see this described in some of the paediatric reports you may have. Children with RAD have extreme and inappropriate social interactions and behavioural issues. These children have missed out on having their early (so pre-5 years of age) emotional and physical care needs met which is basically from a lack of a stable caregiver, a lack of attachment, and a chaotic and abusive environment.

RAD expresses itself in children in different presentations: inhibited children, these are children that are emotionally withdrawn and will not seek comfort or attention and disinhibited children these are the children that appear to be overly outspoken bordering on aggressive, demanding attention and affection from anyone.

Other researchers found that these children had more behavioural problems, social issues, were more withdrawn; had more somatic issues, anxiety/depression, cognitive and attention problems, lacked empathy and exhibited aggressive behaviours. Whoah! And get this; there is no form of treatment that is proven to work for these little ones.

Let's get down to business — how do you raise children with insecure attachments? Firstly, you must understand what attachment is and do some reading and research to figure out what attachment style your child has and

then you may be able to employ the right strategies to develop and form the child's attachment to you.

Rebuilding attachment structures can be called scaffolding which basically understands that the brain is flexible and able to heal (the scientific term is neuroplasticity) and employing appropriate strategies to reform attachment. We know that children who have insecure attachments will have problems with their emotional, cognitive and behavioural development and, as previously discussed, this produces huge difficulties with peer relationships and establishing long-term secure attachments to caregivers. When we see inappropriate behaviours we need to respond with the idea that this child is hurt and frightened and not just misbehaving. We also know that this may take years and years for you, dear carer, to support the repair so a child has the ability to connect with others.

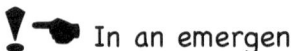 In an emergency

- If you are in a social situation or public environment, remove the child when they begin to display inappropriate behaviour and ensure the child is safe.
- Keep your tone light and try not to engage at their level of anguish.
- Speak clearly and verbalise that they need to stop what they are doing.
- Tell them what the consequence is for their behaviour when they are calm.
- As soon as possible after the incident do an activity together to re-establish connection.
- Use any strategy from your tool kit such as sensory items, cold water play, a breathing exercise, stomping and bringing them back into the moment.
- Engage their senses, name what they can see, point to 5 blue items, what do you smell, what do you hear, what is your stomach doing, are you hungry.
- Keep a hankie in your pocket with scented oil or something to play with.

Chapter 7   Attachment

Prevention strategies

Dr Daniel Hughes is the rockstar of treating children with attachment issues, buy his books, check him out on YouTube and TED talks, go and see him if you can. Dr Dan has some great books explaining the complexity of attachment and he has come up with a very simple but effective treatment for attachment. This is known as 'PACE' communication with children. By the way Dr Dan is a clinical psychologist not actually a rockstar pumping out come cool riffs and hip tunes in a leather-clad funk band, though not sure what he does in his spare time!

How does PACE work?

P — Playfulness

Dr Dan suggests creating an environment of relaxation, this includes your body language such as a lightness in your tone, the way you hold yourself and also within the home environment. And it is mostly about having fun, laughing, smiling and being positive — obviously not being a clown all the time, just being light and cheerful. The aim of playfulness is to help a child regulate their emotions, manage their feelings, give hope, support and encouragement to the development of the child's sense of humour. Humour adds resilience to a child's emotional world. Humour is the fastest way to diffuse a difficult situation. Check out the movie *Patch Adams*. If you struggle with humour put some movies on that are funny and laugh at the funny bits even if you have seen the movie 101 times. This teaches by way of role modelling what's accepted as funny.

A — Acceptance

As with a healthy secure attachment, unconditional love and acceptance gives a child a sense of safety. The big thing here is to accept the child no matter what the behaviour is like. That doesn't mean condoning the behaviour it just means understanding and not judging the behaviour or approaching the child as a 'naughty child'. Knowing if a child is reacting from inner affect dysregulation and is fearful, worried, hurt or sad can help the carer support the child instead of getting caught up in the behaviour. Consequences are about the behaviour not the child. I have come across a few carers that continually belittle their children saying 'Well, they should get it by now', 'They should not do this or that', 'They should know better'

— this says more about the carer's ignorance and lack of self-awareness than the child's ability to heal. The aim is to develop a child's self-worth by accepting them. If you can take anything away from this please stop assuming that the child knows how to 'behave' properly.

C — Curiosity

Being curious about the child and the child's behaviour is essential. This helps the carer make sense of how the child has learnt to behave and we can then become aware of what, how and why they are behaving in this way. Being curious also helps the child see that you are not judging them as this judgment will increase the child's shame. Simply witnessing them, being responsive and supportive by being curious lessens your anger reactions and reduces the child's shame and fear triggers. This can eventually lead to a reduction of inappropriate behaviour.

E — Empathy

Having empathy for the child shows the child that they are super important to you, that you will be there for the child no matter what and can understand what is going on for them.

Some other little hints on attachment

- Knowledge is critical and essential.
- Have several appropriate consequences at hand as this will make stressful times easier to manage.
- Have a script memorised to repeat when the child is displaying inappropriate behaviour. This will make the situation easier to manage and gives you something to focus on as your own distress increases. For example, 'Come on then Jo we can't hurt ourselves or others. Let's get off the floor and go for a walk/drink/outside'. 'Your behaviour was scary for T and I bet you felt scared too, how about after you clean up we play a game of cards, I will help you tidy up'.
- Acknowledge and praise good choices and behaviour for example 'Jo seemed to have a great time when you shared your toys today'.
- When you give a consequence to a child start with 'I am disappointed' or 'I am sad that you did ...'.

- Have a friend that you can rely on for support.
- Routine and predictable environment makes for a less stressful life.
- Keep your discussions simple especially with requests and explanations. How do you eat an elephant? One bite at a time.
- Use appropriate quick, short, sharp consequences, time inside and supervised. We have to teach these children how to regulate.
- Use fun, creative, humour, calm and be light.
- Don't argue and don't buy into the child's need to control the situation.

How to build attachment

- Find an activity to do together such as ukulele lessons.
- Play together, read together, sing and dance together.
- Go for walks together and talk about things you see.
- Talk about your day and your feelings.
- Draw, paint, create together — there are loads of websites that have cool craft activities that don't cost heaps.
- Cook together.
- Take naps together.
- Tidy the house together, kids (well, little ones) love to be helpful and it's a great way to praise their success, behaviour and ability.

I completely bang on about this with carers and parents — no matter how the child behaves you are the adult that they love, you are the one they need in their life. PLEASE take some time each week to spend some one-on-one time with your child. Whether it is a milkshake on a Friday arvo, a drive to sport (yep, there it is again sport, sport, sport) on Saturday morning, or simply a PJ day playing in the house and chatting about things without any pressure.

This is directly from Dr Dan

> The Power of Empathy
>
> With empathy, when the child is sad or in distress the adult is feeling the sadness and distress with her and lets the child know that.
>
> The adult is demonstrating that he or she knows how difficult an experience is for the child. The adult is telling the child that she will not have to deal with the distress alone.
>
> The adult will stay with the child emotionally, providing comfort and support, and will not abandon her when she needs the adult the most.

(extracted from https://ddpnetwork.org/about-ddp/meant-pace/)

The adult is also communicating strength, love and commitment with confidence that sharing the child's distress will not be too much. Together they will get through it.

Chapter 8

Family contact

Steep learning curve here we come! 'Contact must be in the best interests of the child'*, says the Family Court of Australia. Family contact is probably the most difficult situation that carers have to deal with and, let's face it, you can see the impact on the child before, during and after contact and especially if parents fail to attend. You will also face pressure from agencies with regards to the frequency, duration, the times, transport and delegation of duties around the contact.

At times you will probably feel unsupported and frustrated by the many factors that influence birth family contact. But mostly you will be left at home scratching your head and freaking out about the response your child is displaying.

So why is contact important? Not only is contact important it is pretty much essential for a child. A child has the right to have contact with their birth parents, to know who they are and to have the opportunity to ask questions about their family history. This allows for insight into family

---

* http://www.familycourt.gov.au

dynamics and this supports the development of identity. Our responsibility as adults is to keep these vulnerable children safe and to allow them the space to talk about their experience and dispel any magical thinking. It is our responsibility to be compassionate and empathic and not judging or demeaning. Contact comes in many forms and sometimes it is left up to the carer to encourage and advocate for the child to retain important relationships.

Senior social work researchers Elsbeth Neil and David Howe (2004, p. 239) explain the purpose of contact with birth parents as helping children to meet three basic developmental needs which are:

1. achieving good mental health
2. resolving issues of loss and trauma,
3. achieving a strong sense of person.

These do happen when the child has a secure relationship with nurturing carers that are aware that contact supports identity formation and connectedness which allows for the three needs to be achieved.

The behaviour that you will observe after birth family contact can differ from hyperarousal to shutdown and withdrawal but underlying all of the child's responses and behaviour is emotional dysregulation (remember that?) caused by emotional and psychological triggers, triggers from past trauma memories and triggers from fear. This is when you will be questioning the importance of contact, you will be thinking 'wow one step forward and seven back!', you will wonder how can you send your child, who is really starting to settle and make some progress, into a situation with people that neglected them, starved them, took drugs when they were pregnant with them… the list goes on. Well you just do and you support your child through their process.

How do you manage the child's response? Don't take it personally! Most carers want to protect their child from further instability and hurt feelings and hate to see their child distressed. Whilst most contact is supervised, in some situations supervision is transferred to the carer to undertake once safety is established.

The bigger contact strategies

- Be prepared and informed. Know the details of the contact plan as decided on by the court.

- Understand what has led the child to be removed and discuss prior contact visits with the caseworker to get some background information. This is when you should be a pain in the butt as the more information you have from the caseworker the better you can prepare yourself, your child and your family.

- Understand that birth parents are grieving in their own way, they are feeling the shame and loss and perhaps guilt.

- *Don't take it personally.* As a carer you will have to respond to allegations made by parents. Understand where they are coming from, reframe your thinking and take the message that you are doing the right thing. Talk to the caseworkers and be open and honest. This

- is just part of the process and isn't it good that they are caring for your child by checking things out.

- Most birth parents need to feel that they have a say in the child's life so may make complaints about your level of care. Take this in your stride and say to yourself, 'Isn't it good that the parents care for their child and want to make sure he/she is safe and happy' — you can work with that.

- Talk to your child about the contact and explain how their parents might be feeling.

- After contact your child may be a bit ratty and either hyperactive or withdrawn so the focus is to bring the child back into their new world and into their safe home quickly — work through the behaviours.

- Work into the conversation that they are safe, that they might feel sad, scared, angry which are all healthy things to feel and they have done nothing wrong, the fact they are not able to live with their parents is not their fault.

- Tell them 'Mum and Dad love you very much but find it very difficult to care for you the way you need to be looked after and that is now my job to keep you safe and looked after'.

- The sooner you build connection with the birth family the sooner things will be bearable for everyone concerned. For children to experience their two families establishing a respectful relationship and working together is pretty powerful and healing. It's all about the kids right!

In an emergency

- After contact and before going home, go to an oval or park for a run around or swing, take the dog for a walk or even go for a quick swim or to a lookout.

- Jump on a trampoline, get a hot chocolate after contact.

- Make an 'after contact' ritual.

- If appropriate ask open questions such as 'How did everything go?' This can help to develop memory. You can ask things like the temperature of the room they were having contact in, the weather, what colour top Mum or Dad was wearing, had they changed their hairstyle, what was the child's favourite part of the visit.

- Buy a journal and between visits encourage the child to write or draw things for their parents. This can then be taken to contact and provides subjects for the parents to talk about as the child will probably not be able to recall anything they have been doing due to their emotional arousal.

- Send snacks and water just in case. Mostly parents are asked to provide food however sometimes they are unable to do so. In these cases provide the feast as it is not the child's fault if parents don't bring food; don't punish the child. The caseworker can raise this issue with parents and sometimes it works.

- Provide a feedback diary as this will help develop the relationship between parents and carers. Add photos and jot down notes about how the child is going. You can even ask them questions to encourage them to still feel part of the care of the child, for example, 'Does Jo like white or brown bread better?' or 'What was Jo's favourite TV show?'. While the parents may initially be defensive try and let it go, people change over time.

- Just like parents that divorce the healthier the relationship between the parents the better the outcome is for the child and this removes pressure off the child to choose which one they like better.

- Kids love looking at old photos of themselves and they love hearing about little things they did growing up. A diary you send to the contact allows you to ask some questions, fills in the blanks and takes away shame. This can allow the parent to recall positive memories of the child and write them down in the diary. This exercise can also prepare the parent for the next visit with more memories.

- Ask the child what similarities they have with their parent. Ask them do you have same smile, the same laugh, the same colour eyes or hair or the same walk.

Prevention strategies

- Contact must always be in the best interests and be enjoyable for the child — (oh yeah, I said that).
- Life story work is really good for everyone as it builds attachment, gives a narrative and witness to the child's life, and reduces shame and fear.
- Add contact information to life story work.
- Get information about the broader family and if it is appropriate to establish contact with them that you can supervise. Even if it's meeting at a park every now and then.
- Seriously, shit happens. Contact workers are late or cancel, and parents may cancel. Don't tell the child that contact is going to happen until either the night before or morning of.
- If parents are transient ask the caseworker to have the parent confirm attendance at least 24 hours prior to contact so that you minimise any unnecessary stress on the child. That's not to say they might still pull a no-show but this can reduce some of the stress for the child.
- Always check with the caseworker what is appropriate but if it is safe establish emails or letters even if they have to go through the caseworker or the carer.
- Encourage continued contact with friends from the child's previous school, either through visits or email.
- Understand and be careful of social media and have very clear rules around this.
- Make sure you buy gifts for the parents for special occasions. And discuss with the caseworker to remind the parents about birthdays and special events to give them the opportunity to bring a gift. Send birthday cards on time to parents if allowed.
- Try to separate the parent's behaviour from the actual relationship you are trying to establish. Did I mention 'Don't take it personally'.
- Talk about the parents at home in a very simple way, not too much but a little after contact just to ease the child back into his or her safe

Chapter 8   Family contact

world. Be curious but don't interrogate. If you need information ask the caseworker and, of course, out of earshot of your child.

- If you are a relative carer then your job has that extra layer of complexity and it is important to manage your boundaries and your own mental health, speak to the caseworker, attend a support group or get some support with a counsellor.
- Always ask yourself what is good for the child. It is your job to advocate on your child's behalf.
- If contact occurs in a corrections facility still encourage the sharing of journals and paintings but keep out personal details as this ensures the child is protected but the content is okay.
- Make sure you find out from the agency what is appropriate to share.
- Get the child to take activities with them like a game of Uno or a pack of cards, colouring in or a book to read.
- Help make a ritual for the parent and child to increase the positive contact.
- The more positive the contact for the child the less behaviour you will have to deal with.

- *Boundaries* — if you have any concerns after contact talk to the caseworker straight away and put it in an email. It is always important to have a paper trail as life gets busy and we tend to forget things.
- Caseworkers are great at playing 'bad cop' when discussing boundaries with parents and these can include what parents can and shouldn't discuss with the child or simply what food is preferred.

Chapter 9

Toilet issues (eek!)

Did you know that most children who enter care were never properly toilet trained? Many children that were neglected have never learnt to wee or poo using a toilet, and if the child has any developmental issues this adds further problems to toileting. Some children that have a history of neglect and trauma were kept in nappies well past the appropriate time to be toilet trained. Some children may have developed physical responses to stress such as constipation and/or diarrhoea, soiling themselves and bed wetting. These behaviours are common for children with significant trauma as they simply don't have a healthy relationship with their body. For example, the cramps that children feel when needing to do a number two may feel painful and uncomfortable so the child holds on creating a cycle of urge, pain and constipation.

What are you faced with:

- Enuresis is basically bed-wetting after an age that the child should be toilet trained.
- Encopresis is soiling (or the clinical term — pooing or dumping) usually in places that are not really cut out for this such as on the

floor, in a wardrobe or even on your lounge, after the usual age for toilet training.

How do you deal with enuresis and encopresis? (Well, firstly, you begin with trying to pronounce the words. When you have done that let me know — I kind of mumble over them myself.)

First things first is to understand your child's background and also consult with your GP or paediatrician to rule out any medical conditions such as chronic constipation or any urinary tract infections. Once this is done and you find that the issue is behavioural then you can try some of the following strategies. Consider that your child may not think this is a big issue and may try and hide the evidence or get cranky if you try and address it with them. For most children the feeling of shame is real and these toileting behaviours exacerbate negative feelings so it is important for you to keep patient. Punch a pillow and/or gag later but in front of your child breathe (probably not through your nose) and be serene.

Some children with attachment issues feel unlovable and this may translate to the child being fearful of connecting to their new carer. I am not sure that a child is able to think this out but I do think that the child's fear of connection is so high and so uncomfortable that they want to push carers away

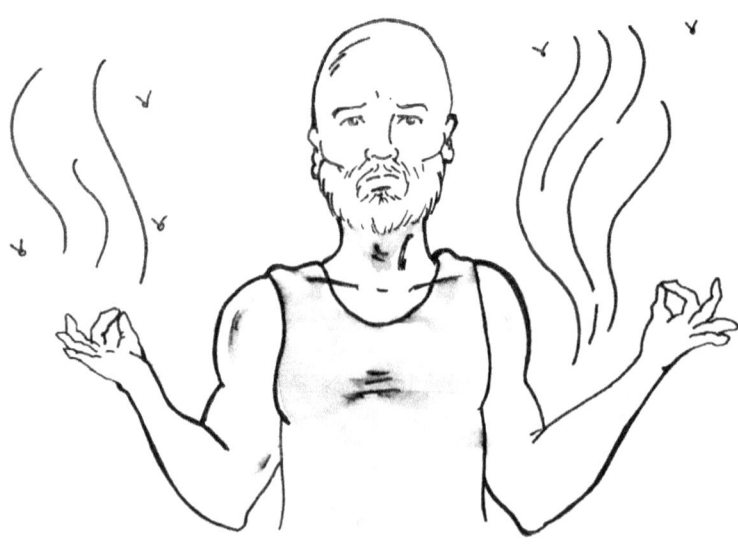

especially if the action or behaviour they use gets the type of attention that reinforces their self-loathing. Not only do enuresis and encopresis become behavioural issues but so can other hygiene issues such as refusal to shower or bath, brushing teeth, wearing clean clothing, and hiding food or rubbish in their bedroom until the smell knocks you over.

Let's talk statistics to get some perspective — most children can control their bowels before their bladder (around 2–4 years old). Around 2 to 3 years of age most children can control their bowels throughout the day and night. Some children that become toilet trained will still require pull up pants overnight. Be aware that research suggests most abuse happens around the toilet training age so the bathroom may be a traumatic trigger for some children. The bathroom can be a place where bad things happened and this deeply impacts on a child's development.

In an emergency

- Always keep clean undies, wipes and clean clothes at hand.
- Keep the above at school and discuss any of the issues with a trusted teacher and office staff.
- Deal with the smelly (showers, baths and clean linen and clothes).
- Teach the child how to use your toilet, where the flush button is, where the loo paper is kept and always keep a bucket of water next to the loo for dirty undies.
- Prepare a script and a consequence that is your 'go to' for these events.
- Prepare for social occasions so you don't miss out.
- Talk about yourself — when you need to go to the loo, for example, say 'I need to go to the toilet before I wet my pants….'.
- Try and come up with a word or sign for when the child needs to go to the toilet so they don't have to actually ask but can give the sign like pulling an earlobe. This takes away the shame plus makes it fun. Make sure to let the teacher in on this.

- If an accident occurs don't accept excuses for this behaviour for example, 'I didn't mean to rub poo all over the beanbag it happened because the dog scared me'. How about saying, 'Let's not talk about the "why" you did it but while we clean it up together let's talk about "how" we can prevent it from happening again. What could we do? Without overreacting, try to get the child to help clean up the mess.

- Work out a plan together if you are going out — so supermarkets, friend's houses after school, soccer training (sport again, groan), or any regular activity. This will increase the child's awareness; they may feel safe having a plan and will support your relationship as you are open with them when discussing loo stuff.

- `Don't blame or shame but talk about it like it's no problem.

- Ask the child each day if they have done a poo or used the loo. Keep a diary so you can have a record — good for the paediatrician, to prevent constipation and to see any behaviour patterns or improvements. However, you don't need to stand at the bathroom door diarising their bowel movements in front of them; it's more as a record for yourself. My kids used to get sick of me asking them 'did you do a poo today — yes — great work!'.

- Set down specific times during the day and before bed to use the bathroom. Stop drinks around 2 hours before bed. Say that we all need to go to the loo before bed that's what we do.

- It's about 20 minutes after a child has eaten that they may need to go to the toilet. Try and encourage the child to sit on the throne twice a day for about 5 to 10 minutes after the 20 minutes is up, preferably at the same time each day so after breakfast and after dinner.

- For constipation encourage a child to sit on the toilet and blow like they are blowing candles out. This is the same physical feeling as pushing and using a footstool allows the child to relax the stomach muscles.

- Make the dunny fun, put up some funny pictures or have a basket that has some small toys (don't worry it won't be for long). Put some books or mags in there or have music on near the bathroom so they can listen to it.

- Get your child to help you clean the bathroom and choose the toilet paper, the shampoo, handwashing soap and the towels to help give them some control on the space.

Chapter 9   Toilet issues

- Let the child know when the cleaning or toilet time is done it will be TV time, nap time, snack time or they can keep playing outside with the dog. Keep them present.

Prevention strategies

- Talk about it, tell them when you need to go to the loo, say things like 'We just drank so much water do you need to go because I sure do'. Tell them when you are off to do a poo. Tell them you get some cramps or do lots of farts which means 'uh oh poo alert'.

- Ask the child what signs their body gives. One of my lovely counselling colleagues always gets the children she does therapy with to ask their bladder or their bowel how it's feeling, 'Hey there bowel/bladder do you need to go to the toilet?' This is a great way for the child to feel if they need to go and to make it fun.

- Children with toileting issues can be smelly so you must encourage washing and showering — bribes work.

- Draw stick figures to have visual diagrams to put on the toilet wall to show the steps:

    1. Pull down pants
    2. Sit on toilet
    3. Flush toilet
    4. Pull up pants
    5. Wash hands

- Prevention does not just involve preventing accidents it also involves preventing shame. Conversations in the home need to include siblings and/or family members to educate them on why this is a normal response for some children and how you are going to address this. It may be useful to include in the house rules that discussing particular issues outside of the family home will result in an age appropriate consequence.

- Good communication with teachers is also important and to work out an accident action plan such as the teacher organises toilet breaks

- for all kids, reminders are given to the entire class, and the teacher is the go-to person if an accident occurs and holds the spare undies.

- Move towards independence by keeping spare undies in a plastic bag in their school bag.

- Maybe use pull ups when particularly stressful events are coming up and talk to the child. Some older kids freak out when you mention a pull up, however, why not talk about the fact that the reason pull ups exist and in such large quantities is because so many kids need them and wear them, that other kids don't advertise it, they just don't talk about it.

- I have heard of reward systems and star charts and this may be successful but, really, tell me someone who actually does this and follows through with it on a daily basis. Let's find quicker and easier solutions.

- Praise your child but don't go over the top as this can create embarrassment.

- Encourage your child by saying not to worry it won't take long until you have this.

- Therapy can help a child to process the prior traumatic events.

- Do some psycho-education about how the body works and the more people talking about this openly lessens the impact of the hiding.

- Then there is the wiping and washing education. You can use dolls and play with them — or maybe even cars need to do a wee.

The foundation of toileting success is the home structure and healthy routines such as good sleep, healthy diet, regular exercise, safety and acceptance and a predictable environment these all support a child's emotional, mental and physical wellbeing. Hydration encourages weeing and pooing and a good diet keeps a child regular. Ensure the child has daily showers or baths, and encourage and praise good hygiene practices.

When all else fails — Go back to basic toilet training, teach children about getting to know their body — teaching kids awareness on how their body feels, how these little guys know when they need to go to the loo. The following illustrations can help with this.

Chapter 9   Toilet issues

Follow the poo

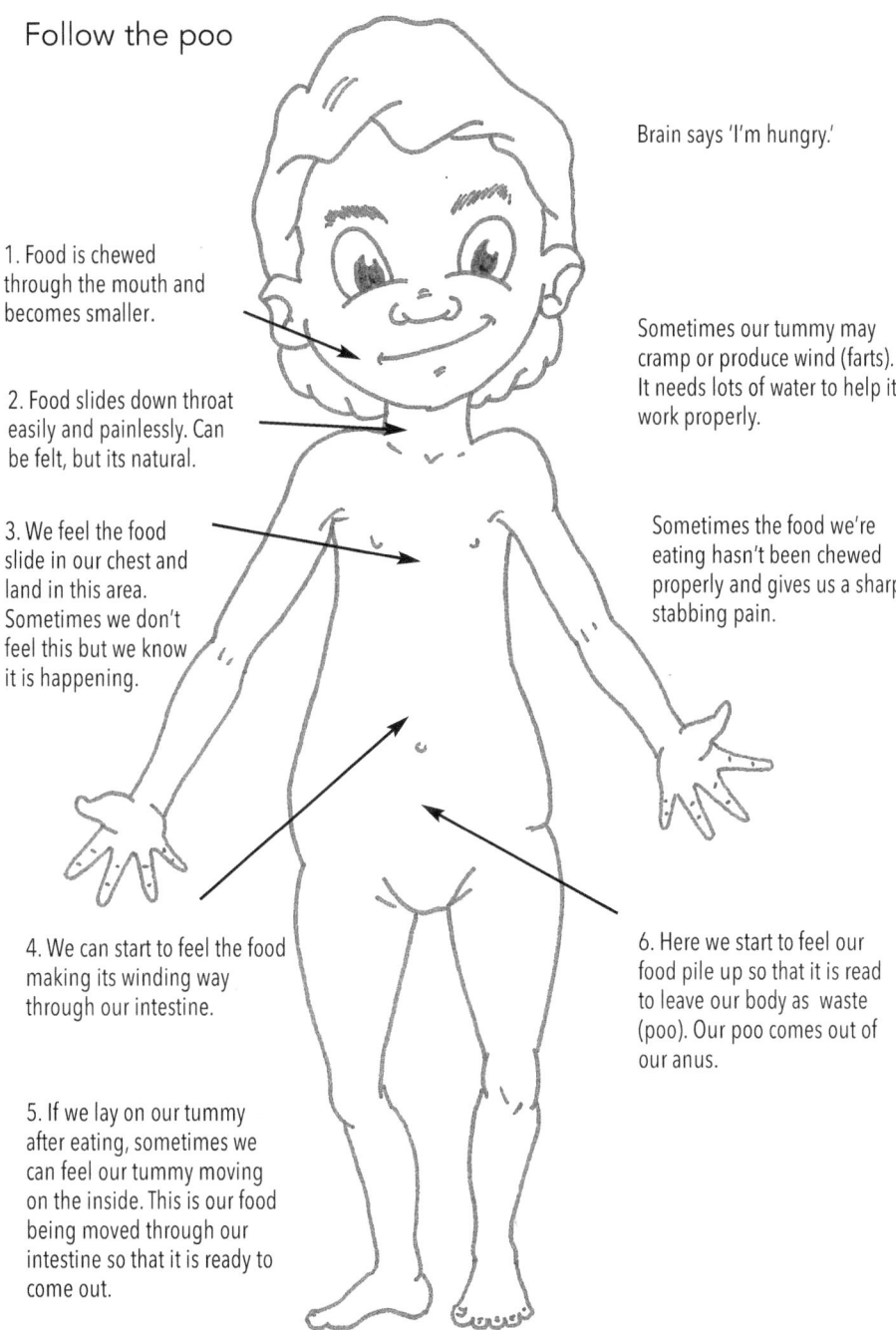

Brain says 'I'm hungry.'

1. Food is chewed through the mouth and becomes smaller.

2. Food slides down throat easily and painlessly. Can be felt, but its natural.

Sometimes our tummy may cramp or produce wind (farts). It needs lots of water to help it work properly.

3. We feel the food slide in our chest and land in this area. Sometimes we don't feel this but we know it is happening.

Sometimes the food we're eating hasn't been chewed properly and gives us a sharp stabbing pain.

4. We can start to feel the food making its winding way through our intestine.

6. Here we start to feel our food pile up so that it is read to leave our body as waste (poo). Our poo comes out of our anus.

5. If we lay on our tummy after eating, sometimes we can feel our tummy moving on the inside. This is our food being moved through our intestine so that it is ready to come out.

7. Our brain tells us when our poo is ready to come out.

8. Our anus is here, in the middle of our bum. When we are ready to poo our tummy cramps slightly and our bum muscles tighten. This tells us that our anus muscles are ready to push out our poo.

9. After we have gone to the toilet and pooed we have to wipe our bum. To do this we roll or scrunch up some toilet paper and bend our arm behind us, place the toilet paper on our anus and wipe with some force. Not so much that it hurts, but enough to know that it is being cleaned.

10. Repeat step 9 and check toilet paper for brown or green (depending on what you ate) colour. Only when the toilet paper comes back clean with no colour after wiping can you stop this and flush the toilet.

11. Now wash hands. To do this properly we have to rinse our hands with water, apply soap in a thick layer and scrub our hands together for 3 seconds. We then rinse our hands again for the time it takes you to sing 'Happy Birthday' in your head.

12. Dry hands with paper or a hand towel.

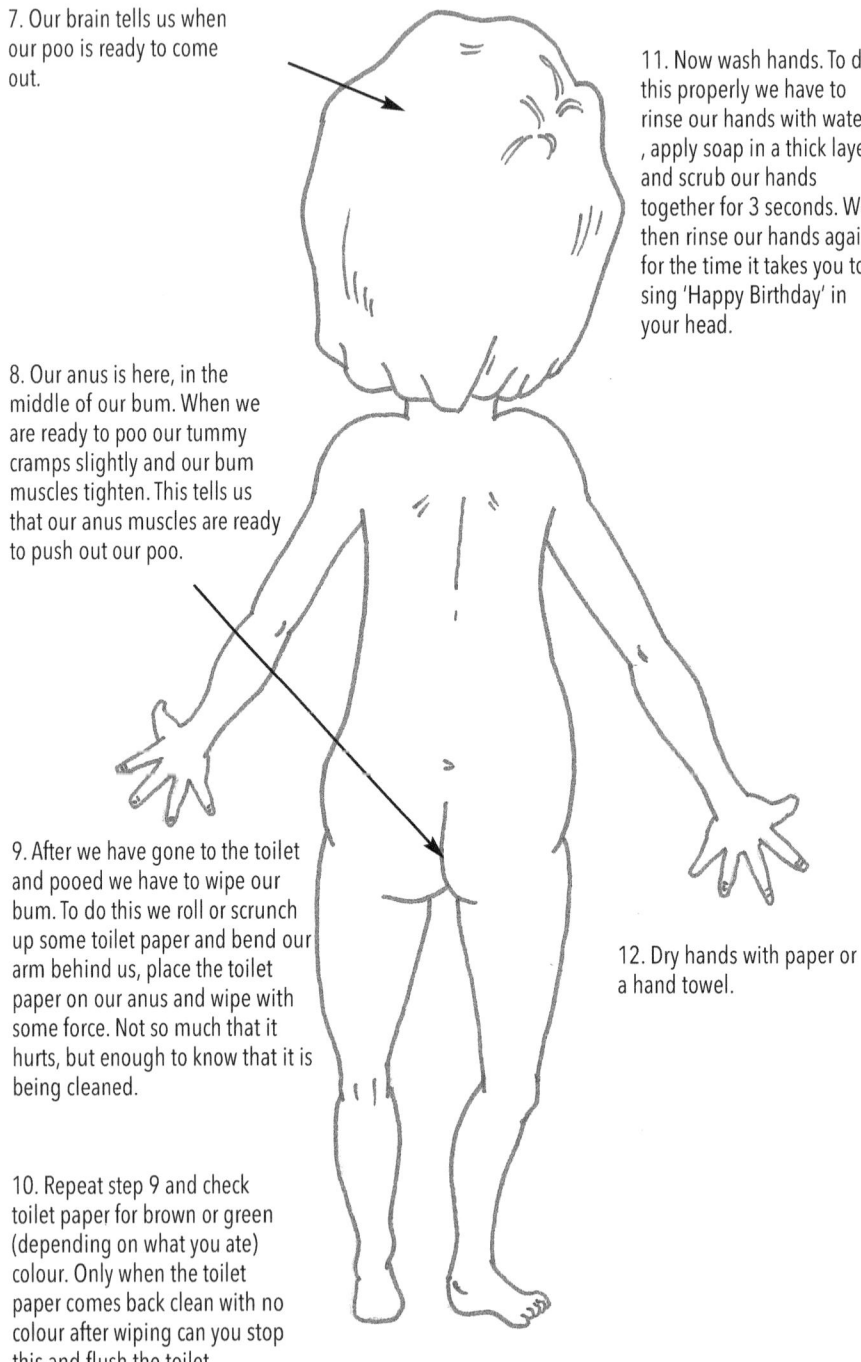

Chapter 10

Eating habits

At some point children can become fussy eaters and this is mostly true for children with autism and developmental delays. However, those children that have complex trauma may have eating issues. Some children have never experienced rich or varied food and without judgment many of these children that have endured neglect or chaotic environments have been raised on processed, high-sugar and high-fat content food and mostly no regular mealtimes.

It's important to take your time to understand the child and their unique background and to slowly work towards introducing new foods, flavours and textures in the child's diet. For some children their only attachment or memory is the food they have eaten with their birth family. For example chicken nuggets may have been the main food that the parents ate with the child or the child was taught to make for their siblings so removing this from their diet immediately isn't okay. Instead make it an occasion like every Friday night for a time.

There are many reasons children avoid eating but it's important that you understand the 'why' and good luck to you. Firstly, find out if there is an organic issue, such as discomfort from eating, reflux, gagging, stomach pain, and/or incorrect chewing methods. Sore teeth or inadequately formed dental or gum problems and medication may reduce appetite.

Did you know that eating is difficult — can you believe that? Wish that was my case when a Tim Tam comes my way. There are complex physical and sensory systems at work, not to mention coping with textures, tastes and anxiety when eating. Some highly anxious kids don't like having full tummies as it makes them feel uncomfortable. Then there is gorging food, stealing and hiding food. This can happen due to a child never knowing when they will get their next meal or if there is never enough food available for their growing body. How do you help? Time and patience.

In an emergency

- Try juices and smoothies. Use rice malt syrup or dextrose as a sweetener as it is easier for the child to digest.
- Engage a teacher to keep lunchbox and teach giving out recess and then lunch.
- Use a plain cup, plate and bowl to begin with so eating is not a sensory overload.
- If there are any issues allow the child to use fingers and hands to eat and slowly introduce cutlery.
- Don't stress too much in the beginning, the child may be uncomfortable at the table so allow them to eat under the table or everyone can sit on the floor as a picnic and slowly work towards the goal you would like to achieve.
- When a baby eats they squish food and jam it in their mouth — for a while make it fun.
- Use music and change the environment.
- Have things to play with like a Lego figure to distract from the texture of the food.

- Use a picture of having a full tummy. Talk about it, 'My tummy is full, I am hungry because my belly is making weird noises, how do we fill it up'.

Prevention strategies

- Cook, work out a menu plan, grocery list and shop together if your child is able to manage.
- Slowly introduce different vegies, salad and fruit over time as the child's digestive system may not be used to this.
- Paediatricians or dieticians are great to get information from.
- Give the child control. Look through recipe books together, find a healthy option and a non-healthy option and make both; such as lasagne and chocolate cupcakes.
- Go back to early childhood strategies to make food basic and easily digestible and then slowly add to it.
- Mouth skills such as chewing can be taught by a dietician and an occupational therapist.
- Be prepared again as food time can be stressful so watch your language. Don't allow the child to throw food around the table but say things like 'Your food can stay on your plate' rather than 'Don't throw your food'.
- Set meal times – ROUTINE, ROUTINE AND MORE ROUTINE!
- Use easy food to eat at school.
- Encourage control.
- Use sauces and gravy and slowly decrease.
- Give vitamins such as fish oil and vitamin C.
- Magnesium is great for sleep and for good digestion. Talk to your paediatrician or GP about these supplements as they are good for the nervous system.
- Always have a bowl of fruit or a fruit plate on the table so the child can take some as they need it

- Keep a box of snacks in the pantry that the child can have access to at all times.
- Keep asking if they would like a snack, like a piece of toast, a bit of fruit, cheese and crackers. This will help them know that food is constantly provided.

Chapter 11

Lying and stealing

I can hear you shaking in your boots. Is this going to get worse with each section? What else do we have to deal with? You may well be asking 'why am I doing this?' Well, I have no idea why you are but good on you for caring for a unique and beautiful child that needs to be safe and deserves to have the very best life from here on in.

Let's cut to the chase. Kids that are dealing with complex trauma steal and lie. Yep, there it is, most kids steal but those little ones that have come from these backgrounds do it more and they do it for longer probably for around two years longer and it can appear any time the child is feeling unsafe.

Why? Usually stealing and lying is about safety, control and survival. These children have learnt these skills to survive, and they are not manipulating, by lying they are probably hoping they are not going to get into trouble. Most importantly these children need to be treated respectfully and compassionately.

By understanding the child's brain we are able to bring a sense of calmness to our interaction with the child. We need to understand that these children just don't get the 'cause and effect' thinking and will not 'learn from their mistakes', any consequence that involves 'you did this so your consequence is...' just doesn't work. Consequences need to be given calmly, with humour and they are to be quick and explained clearly. What the big picture is here is moral development through attachment and safety.

While lying and stealing are normal for all children, you may find that this issue is more ongoing for children from trauma backgrounds. Moral or conscience development occurs naturally at different stages in life and generally from learning cause and effect. Children who have poor cognitive development lack the ability to understand cause and effect and their moral development is delayed. This means they know lying and stealing is wrong but don't have the 'care' factor accompanying the act. Stealing — a five year old is not going to rack off with your family car or your superannuation but they may nick something pretty and precious or it may just be food. School teachers may notice things being taken; peers lose food or stationery,

siblings may find their electronic devices gone. This child can stand there with chocolate ice cream all over their face and in their hair and swear on your life they have not been taste testing.

Some kids that have attachment issues (see info on attachment in Chapter 7) go into survival mode and take things as a way of feeling whole and 'fitting in' with their peers. Children who were not taught to have personal boundaries and have had their own violated may believe that it is acceptable to enter someone else's space and take things. So to get your head around this — kids that grow up in families that steal or where they have had to lie and steal to survive, well, this behaviour becomes normal and it can allow them to feel some sort of attachment to their parents.

Everyone bangs on about natural and logical consequences but what are they — natural consequences are the experience that naturally occurs after a certain behaviour or decision. Going to school on a cold day without a jumper and the natural consequence is the child will be cold. It is important that children have these experiences as they will learn that actions do have consequences which lead to healthy choices. Logical consequences are those that are chosen by carers or teachers that follow unacceptable behaviour such as if the child physically assaults another child at school they may be suspended and have to discuss this with the principal.

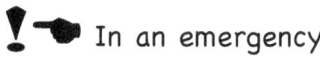 In an emergency

- Take a step back, pause, breathe and then repeat over and over, 'this is just a reaction to trauma' and do this for the next 5 years.

- When a child steals from a shop, friend or sibling as quickly as possible take the child with you to return the item, hand it over to the person or if a shop the manager or checkout person and apologise for taking the item. This isn't about shaming or blaming, it's a natural consequence.

- Don't try and find out the WHY, you already know this. Ask for the WHAT — what did you want that for? What was happening before you took it? How did you feel in your body before and after? What do you think we do now?

- Give the child time — ignore the lie, reassure and say something like 'We need to talk about this at some point, I will wait for you to be ready to talk about this, and I know what happened so when you're ready we will talk about this'.

- When they are ready, focus on the behaviour and the effects of the behaviour.

- Watch your language — use phrases like 'I feel disappointed and/or sad'. Don't use 'angry'.

- Let the child know what they can do differently and give them choices. They can ask to touch, play or borrow an item.

- Have a script, list of jobs and consequences at the ready.

- Let them know you have to tell the teacher and friends and relatives so 'we can manage about the behaviour so we can all work together'.

- Tell them to come for a snack/cuddle/chat/read a book together if they want to steal. Be approachable.

- Start talking about 'cause and effect' using examples in books to teach moral development.

Prevention strategies

- During this time it may be worth storing any valuables in a safe place and encouraging family members to do the same.

- Be open with discussions about the behaviour and focus on the importance of being truthful.

- Let the child know that it is their job to make mistakes, and your job to provide learning, guidance and consequence in order to teach those skills so they learn how to make healthy choices.

- Discuss with the teacher and your social circle how you are approaching this. Education is the key to reducing any shame and blame.

- Have a script and some consequences at the ready and be consistent as this helps in regulating your own emotional reactivity.

- What do you do? The best thing is to lighten up and make a joke such as, 'now why would you be needing this sculpture of Darth Vader, yes, he is cool but he is mine, you can ask to play with it or touch it but it lives in this spot'.

- When it comes to food gently guide the child in the direction of asking for extra if they are hungry and repeating that they will never go hungry in this home and we all have enough food.

- House rules are so good and they can be agreed on by everyone and kept up in a place for all to see. If someone breaks the rules you can point to the house rule and even have a list of consequences. It is important they understand this by way of role play and seeing and doing. Get your other children involved.

- Do a role play on saying sorry and making amends for example, 'I am sorry, can I do your washing up chore tonight'. Then ask them while they are doing it to play their favourite song and once it's done play a game or go for a walk. Give them a future template.

- House rules need to include respecting your own and other people's property and let them know they can do this.

- Teach a child the rules for ownership of property and the boundaries around this including how ownership is transferred. For example, we go to school and all equipment belongs to the school, we can use it, care for it and return it. If we go to the shop items are owned by the shop until we buy them then they are ours.

- Understand this is going to take many years.

- Teach your child how others feel and point it out in books or movies.

- Teaching the difference between borrowing and stealing. Asking and then giving back can also be role played.

Chapter 12

Sexualised behaviour

Okay, let's talk about this — and, yes, it may be uncomfortable, however, you will more than likely come across this behaviour as a carer. It is important that you understand your own sexuality and response to sexualised behaviour as you may feel a little shocked, confused, embarrassed and fearful of how to respond, or quite simply be left gulping for air. I suggest that if these issues occur in your home read up and educate yourself; talk to professionals because if handled empathically and sensitively you can repair so much for the child and reduce the shame a child may have. Handled correctly you can support the development of a healthy sexuality for the child which will include personal boundaries and self-respect.

Learn what normal sexual development and sexual behaviour is as opposed to the sexual behaviour that causes the eyebrows to lift. There are many resources available on this topic, a number of these are listed in the resource section. However, the resource that is well known and easy to understand is the green, orange and red light of sexual behaviour. This guide details age-appropriate behaviours in a clear and easy to understand

format, definitely worth a read. (Just search for "Sexual behaviours traffic light pdf" on the web. There is even an app available).

Basically, sexualised behaviour involves sexual acts that are excessive, occur in an inappropriate environment and there is difficulty distracting the child. Puberty has a lot to do with how the sexualised behaviour is handled. If the behaviour is self-directed and the child has not been through puberty then behaviour is generally seen to be self-soothing, learned behaviour, and in response to trauma. However, if the child has been through puberty and seeks out other children or animals for sexual behaviour then we have a more complex issue that requires loads of intervention with specialised services.

What's appropriate — sexual behaviour is appropriate for any child's development no matter what their age. Sexual behaviour that is curious in nature and may involve play with peers that are roughly the same age and level of development is appropriate. These children can be easily distracted and diverted from the behaviour and this behaviour does not become obsessive or excessive.

What's not appropriate — usually any sexual behaviour that is obsessive, excessive, and mostly self-directed. This is generally a self-soothing behaviour. Areas of concern are when sexual acts, sexual knowledge and sexual language are more advanced and complex for a child of that age, such as the term and act of oral sex.

A little checklist that may help:
- Explicit
- Persistent
- Obsessive
- Involving others
- Compulsive
- Frequency.

Why — while not all children from traumatic backgrounds display sexualised behaviour those children that have witnessed domestic violence, which can include both physical and sexual violence, children that have experienced long-term neglect, and those children that have been a victim of any sexual abuse are more likely to exhibit these behaviours. Mostly sexualised behaviour is learned as a form of comfort and self-soothing, a child can 'act out' sexual knowledge and behaviour in their play, simulating what they have experienced themselves. Alternatively, a child can get 'attention' whether good or bad from this behaviour. Sadly, arousal such as excitement, frustration and confusion, may get confused with sexual urges. A child's body can become physically aroused when they are being held and nurtured and the child becomes confused by these feelings, for example, you may be speaking to a child in a very caring way and you notice they are having an arousal response such as erection, or you may be holding a child and they begin to exhibit signs of arousal and behaviour such as masturbation.

What does it look like — mostly sexualised behaviour is self-directed but the behaviour can impact on other people such as those witnessing the behaviour or those that are being targeted. That means a child may seek out an adult for comfort and begin to behave in sexual manner. The sexual behaviour can be seen in a child's play such as drawing, playing with dolls, or through their language. Inappropriate sexual behaviours are those that are sexual in nature and happen in inappropriate environments such as at school, at a friend's house, or the supermarket. The acts may be masturbation which may or may not result in injury, using implements to insert into their bottom or vagina, trying to touch adults or pets in a sexual manner, using inappropriate sexual language and humping behaviours. Teachers may witness children wiggling around on their bottoms while they are sitting on the floor or leaning up against the corner of tables.

How to manage and cease this behaviour — mostly when the child is in a safe environment with a few basic boundaries much of the behaviour stops. However, you have to act on this behaviour as it is imperative for the child's emotional and psychological health as well as their personal safety. If you do feel out of your depth, and please don't feel bad about this, seek professional support not just for your child but for yourself. It is important to find a counsellor that is educated in this as some professionals may not take the behaviour seriously or they may implement harsh punishments that could cause emotional issues and increase feelings of shame.

Then we have social media — read the rules of social media and understand them. Facebook, Instagram, Snapchat, TikTok are the big ones followed by numerous other apps. Children who have difficulty with social connection will find some type of connection through social media and in some ways this is good but mostly it's dangerous. Children from violent and traumatic backgrounds are easy targets, they are easily manipulated and groomed and it doesn't take much for the skilled perpetrator to have kids sending inappropriate information about themselves. You have to be careful with children that are in care as anyone can connect with them such as birth parents or relatives and whilst this may be positive, if allowed it can also have detrimental effects such as undermining the placement, confusing the child and making the child, carers and other family members unsafe.

What do you do? Limits, people — everyone whinges and complains about kids on social media and devices (me too!) but at the end of the day we are the parents and adults and it is our job to protect these vulnerable youngsters. Have you ever read the terms and conditions of specific social media platforms? Do you know the age that the app is recommended for?

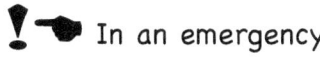 In an emergency

- Keep the child safe and remove the child from the public place, however, don't throw them over your shoulder and run screaming through Big W, instead, gently direct them out the door firmly but caringly whilst holding your breath and screaming silently.
- Talk to the teachers — have a team at school ready to act with a clear plan to add to the consistency. Be specific and consistent with script 'okay children, hands on knees'.
- DO NOT shame or ask questions as to why they do it, again you already know — and honestly they are probably not even aware they are doing it.
- Give them something to concentrate on such as a lollypop or a sensory item to play with or a scented hankie anything at the ready to distract them with.
- If a child begins to masturbate like no tomorrow try getting them to hold a cold wet facecloth and encourage them to place it on their forehead or behind their neck.
- There may be signs a child displays before engaging in the behaviour. At those times try to manage the arousal appropriately, such as going for a walk, cuddling a teddy, playing with water in a sink or bowl, having a cold drink or getting them to help you outside.
- Always have some items around such as stress balls, a mermaid pillow or some slime to play with.
- Try and do some breathing exercises to regulate the sympathetic side and engage the parasympathetic side. Count evenly as you breathe in and out.
- When you redirect them from the behaviour use the words for exactly what they are doing and how it makes other's feel such as 'Lucy, when you have your hands in your pants it is making me/your classmates very uncomfortable and this is not something you do in public. I want you to stop now and I am going to take you to the sink to wash your hands and play in the water for a bit'.

- Distract with healthy snacks or a cold drink.
- Always use the correct terminology for private parts — mouth, breasts, chest, vagina, penis and bottom. Make language specific.
- Add strategies to the teacher plan.

Prevention strategies

- Knowledge, knowledge and more knowledge of age appropriate sexualised behaviour, the child's past trauma and your own beliefs on sexual behaviour.
- Check out what is triggering the behaviour, for instance, when the child or young person is more likely to act out, such as evening, school, in front of TV. Try and find out what they are getting out of it, do they feel more relaxed are they flooded by triggers and feelings, try and substitute other self-soothing behaviours such as swimming, swings, toys to play with and sensory items.
- Counselling with an appropriate counsellor for both the child and the carer.
- Discuss other people's rights and boundaries and how these discussions are about keeping the child safe.
- Put aside your shame and embarrassment as these children have the right to be safe and to be safe they need to be educated on age appropriate information.
- Use scripts.
- Use the correct words for private parts and sex — yes, penis, penis, vagina, penis and vagina!
- Teach the child the rules for their own body, who can and can't touch, who they can and can't touch and what is appropriate touch.
- Talk about secrets — what is a safe secret (keeping a birthday present a surprise or a friend's crush) and an unsafe secret (where you feel like something is not okay).
- Teach social skills like who they can kiss and hug on greeting and how to greet without physical interaction.

- Teach them about uncomfortable feelings in their belly and what to do when this happens.

- Involve both carers as this is very powerful and healing when you are all comfortable addressing the issue as long as you keep saying it's about safety.

- Social media — keep discussing, have strict limits, don't use as an incentive, make sure that you are on their list as friends, ban all secret accounts that means if the child has a secret account they lose all privileges and NOOOOOO screen stuff in the bedroom.

- Water play, clay play, have things in their pocket like nice-smelling hankies.

- Teach the child about sexual identity and gender roles, and the difference between friendships and relationships.

Before you freak out, most sexual behaviour is easily managed and with clear boundaries generally disappears pretty quickly. Remember these children are vulnerable and are easy targets for predators so keeping an eye on them and their behaviour is important.

SECTION 3

Diving in Deeper

Chapter 13

Boundaries and routines — longer term strategies

Diet

All children require a well-balanced diet. Children that have experienced neglect may have been raised on foods that are not considered healthy and combined with chronic stress and high cortisol levels, has a negative impact on the brain and physical development. A good diet promotes growth, healthy teeth, nails and hair, stimulates and regulates hormone development and is essential to brain development.

Mostly children growing up in adversity are more used to high-sugar, high-fat and high-salt foods that are processed and packaged. Introducing new tastes and food groups can be difficult and even scary for some children. However, if you just relax, go at the child's pace, be inquisitive and go back to basics, you will get there faster with half the resistance.

DON'T

- Don't hide vegetables in foods as this can increase mistrust towards you.
- Don't make dinner too structured in the beginning but work towards a goal to make this achievable.
- Don't create overwhelming meal experiences like seven sets of cutlery or chopsticks if the child is not used to this.
- Don't punish or shame a child around their eating habits.
- Don't use food as a reward or take it away as punishment.
- Don't do the cause and effect talk (for example, 'if you don't eat you will be hungry later and won't sleep').
- Working towards a healthy eating plan can be a full experience and can encourage attachment between the child and the carer.

WHERE TO START

- Have a dental check-up (the child not you).
- Find out if the child is allergic to anything or intolerant to any foods such as lactose or gluten.
- Check your own diet, for example, you may be vegan or vegetarian which may not suit the child so you need to be open to what the child needs before any adjustment in their diet occurs.
- If your own diet is full of packaged and high-salt/sugar diet maybe working with a nutritionist for the family can also align with the child about how you all can eat healthier.
- Be curious ask the child what they like to eat, what their favourite food is, what they like about this food (for example, colour, texture).
- Increase hydration with lots of water. Buy a special water bottle (and 3 spare) and keep it filled during the day to encourage the child to drink or sip water.
- Talk to the child's paediatrician or paediatric dietician regarding supplements; a child with chronic neglect may need extra vitamins and minerals and some of these can be specialised and prescription only.

- Most importantly develop trust and connection and allow them to feel safe in your own home. Hoarding behaviour will decrease when a child is feeling safe.

- Whatever food they like add it to their meal for a time. If the child likes chicken nuggets then start by adding this to the dinner each night reducing the quantity whilst adding other food such as a sliced up chicken schnitzel or sausage or crunchy tofu pieces.

- Understand that food and mealtimes can be very overwhelming for the child and allow them to have some control.

- Get them to pick a plate but try and use plain coloured ones rather than those with patterns.

- Include the child when making, let's say, fries. Show them how a potato can do many things like being mashed, boiled and baked.

- Make meal times predictable and routine.

- Feed snacks regularly throughout the day.

- Go back to basics. When a child is born they drink milk, then porridge, then mashed vegies and soft meats. This is how you do it. Not back to the bottle but just adding soft, mashed vegies with sauces and gravies then work toward reducing these.

- When you start out try to keep food as bland as possible, adding textures they like such as hot chips, use sauces and gravy.

- Try magnesium either as a supplement or add to baths. Magnesium rich foods are really good for anxiety and to help with sleep. Nothing like good old Epsom salts sprinkled in the bathtub.

- By introducing foods slowly your child's little body is more likely to accept them. For example, too many vegies to begin with can fill them full of gas and make them feel uncomfortable. This may then make them want to avoid vegetables.

- If you need a visual, imagine that you are a steak and three veg kinda person and someone puts a really hot vindaloo in front of you — your head nearly explodes and your stomach cramps and you want to escape — how can you eat this, right? Go easy.

- Try to reduce herbs, spices and strong flavours early on and slowly add these as time goes by when the child's taste adapts.
- Having lots of conversation and laughter around the table can distract the child from any distress while they are eating. Even read a book to them at the table.
- Create a ritual, such as 'Friday night pizza night' which can be eaten as a picnic on the floor in front of a good movie.
- Spend some time going through pictures in recipe books and online. Get the child interested in picking food they like the look of, writing a shopping list, making the dish.
- Make it easy for yourself do a menu plan on a Friday evening, groceries on Saturday morning and do some cooking with the kids on Saturday or Sunday afternoon.
- Doing the menu plan with the child and involving them in shopping and cooking gives them a sense of control. Leave the plan on the fridge and ask them: 'So, what are we having for dinner tonight? We better get that out of the freezer to defrost then'. This also lets them know they will be fed and there is a sense of predictability. This may also reduce stealing and hoarding food because they know when the next meal is and what it is. An example of a meal plan is shown on the page opposite.
- Have a snack box somewhere they can reach and where they can get food from without asking plus a fruit bowl or cut up fruit in the fridge for easy access. Maybe do it daily so you can control the amount of food. The contents of a snack box might contain: a piece of fruit, box of sultanas, a packet of chips, popcorn, buttered arrowroot biscuits, nuts, juice or milk, or some homemade choc protein balls. As an emergency snack you might include chewing gum, a lolly to suck on or salt chips.

Children roughly need a snack every two hours to keep up blood sugar levels so if you need to set an alarm on your phone do so and you may also need to discuss this with the teacher. Some schools do *crunch and sip* in class but also to ensure the child has consumed some food during lunch and recess as this time may be overwhelming and not eating will lead to a ratty afternoon.

Chapter 13   Boundaries and routines — longer term strategies

Sample menu plan

	MONDAY	TUESDAY	WEDNESDAY	THURSDAY	FRIDAY	SATURDAY	SUNDAY
Breakfast	Toast	Porridge	Toast	Toast	Toast	Cereal	Eggs Bacon
Lunch	Lunch	Lunch	Lunch	Lunch	Lunch	Lunch	Lunch
Dinner	Spaghetti Bolognese Garlic bread Custard and cake	Dinner	Dinner	Dinner	Dinner	Dinner	Dinner

Sandwich
Fruit
Snack
Extra

NOTE: *I use this system and it works for my family. I have also introduced this system with others that I have worked with. I also know it's bloody difficult to manage everything that life throws at you and sometimes these things slip, well it does for me. Best thing about these ideas is to try them out and see if they help, and you can decide to keep or bin them.*

I am not a nutritionist and I do encourage a healthy balanced diet and the snacks are examples only.

99

Teachers have observed that some children will scoff all their food in the morning before class with nothing left for the rest of the day. If your child is a scoffer maybe ask the teacher to hold the child's lunchbox and give the food out at recess and lunch time. This will encourage routine and allow the child to predict that food is coming their way.

If you aim towards a healthy and balanced diet, including regular snacks and water you will be doing well — take it slow and celebrate success.

Hygiene

Research suggests that most abuse occurs around bathroom time. Children who have this experience may have an aversion to showering, bathing and brushing teeth as well as having toileting issues. Children that have experienced neglect may not be used to regular hygiene practices and might not understand the 'cause and effect' of a lack of good hygiene.

If the goal is to have a child independently taking care of these areas the first step is to establish trust, safety and then to teach the skills necessary for the child to manage these themselves. Children need support with hygiene issues in every social environment, home, school, even at a friend's home. As we know the most important thing is to be consistent and structured for children. Teachers are a great source of support when it comes to routine and consistency (they get it). In my experience, if a teacher is made aware of a child's behaviour and given some clear strategies that mirror and are consistent with yours they are super-cool at following through with these. In fact when they are not operating in the dark and are working with you what will happen for the child is that they are hearing the same message and receiving the same strategy across environments which will speed up this process. When they know what is going on teachers can relax and they can even address some of these issues broadly in the classroom, like washing hands before and after recess, toilet time and lunch time or discussing hygiene issues in circle time.

If the teacher has no idea about complex trauma and is not helpful around these strategies — change classes, the impact of a supportive and caring teacher for these children is incredible, however, if the teacher is not helpful it can further shame the child so get out of there. Keep in mind it is not the teacher's job to parent the child but to assist in the consistency around strategies that you, the carer, bring to them.

Essentially, the child needs to feel a sense of control and safety so they can experience more positive interactions. Whilst they may not be able to verbalise this they will experience new things like being asked to have a play date or attend a birthday party.

The big players in the hygiene arena:

- Dental
- Toileting
- Sexualised behaviour

- Showering/bathing/washing.

The effects of poor hygiene:

- Smelliness
- Unhealthy consequences for oral and physical health
- Possibly being treated differently by teachers and will fly under the radar
- Low self-esteem
- Problems with peers — no one wants to be with the smelly kid
- Possibly at the expense of your carpet.

House rules for hygiene

Establish your house rules, write them up and have all members of the family contribute. Have them on display.

Here's an example of some house rules.

- Wash hands before meals.
- Once a week clean and attend to fingernails and toenails.
- Daily shower or bath.
- Wash basket for dirty clothing.
- Routine for school uniforms, such as a clean one every few days or get changed after school.
- Change sheets weekly or fortnightly.
- Encourage and teach a child how to keep their room clean and organised by providing gentle and consistent guidance.
- New undies and socks daily.
- Brush teeth twice a day.

Other things to consider

- Give the entire family including pets a damn good regular worming treatment.

- Make the rules a conversation topic for the family to talk about and discuss. Ask each other 'Did you brush your teeth, wash your hands' and so on.

- DON'T do *put-downs* even if you're joking like 'Ooohh you don't want to be smelly do you?'. No shame or blame. You wouldn't say this to a baby, would you?

Washing

- How to teach a child to enjoy a shower or bath — *mmm*, well, it's about safety so ask them if they would like you in there with them, sitting outside the bathroom and chatting, just walking up and down the hall singing, or simply leaving the door open a little. They might even want you to leave the door open or sit in with your back to them.

- Be busy and noisy. Chat up and down past the bathroom. Tell them they might not feel safe yet and that's okay, maybe getting them to bath in swimmers or knickers first.

- You will need to teach them how to wash themselves but obviously go easy. Role play how they wash themselves and then encourage them to do the same, especially with boys and foreskins make the conversation easy, so we start with our face then under our arms then our penis or vagina, bottom and then our legs and toes. Make it matter of fact. You could even use dolls to demonstrate.

- Give them some control over their own choice of towel and face washer. They can choose soap and shampoo products.

- Put scented oils in the bathroom or play some music.

- Be warned — some kids will put on the water and not get in to the shower because they are too scared so maybe get them into swimmers and go in with them to teach them.

- Let them know all kids have daily showers or baths and how can 'we' make it a safe and fun time for them. Make it a morning or evening routine.

- Ask them which they prefer a shower or bath. The child may need a bath on weekends if you have to assist washing hair. Throw some toys in the bath or shower for them to play with.

Using the toilet

- Use dolls, picture books and/or role play to teach the child how to wipe and clean themselves. This could make for an interesting sight if the neighbours were looking through your window!
- Keep a bucket next to the toilet for soiled undies.
- Educate the child on how their body feels. See the diagrams in Chapter 9 but come up with your own if you would like to.
- Add some cool funny pictures in the toilet with some toys and magazines.
- Understand the body's timing of poos and wees.
- Ensure good hydration, have their teacher keep a bottle of water on the table.

Dental issues

As touched on earlier, it is important for these children to have regular dental care with an experienced dental technician. The sooner you know if there are going to be any long-term problems the better prepared you are and those conversations can be had. Hygiene is important but if the child is not used to brushing this can be difficult to get into a routine. There are some great little stories you can buy to read and to encourage dental hygiene.

Sometimes you may have to assist in the brushing but keep your eye on it to make sure it's getting done and that they are not just adding a little toothpaste to their mouth to provide the smell factor. Be gentle, gums may be sensitive.

Dentists can be a real trigger for anxiety so be sure to go gently. Visit the dentist and introduce the child to the dentist and facility before attending an appointment. You can use rewards here like a new book after the appointment or bit of Lego as it's a difficult thing to go through.

Don't do a reward chart but you could just do things like say 'I have noticed you have been trying to clean your teeth more this week and so I am going to take you to the movies because that's great work'.

Sexualised behaviour

AWKWARD alert — let's get honest here. A very uncomfortable subject to approach and you may feel inadequate and fearful of offending. Just be open and honest, tell your child you are feeling uncomfortable but 'we' need to talk about this. Children will not tell you what they are doing so it is up to you to name the behaviour and explain how it can make others feel and how it can be unsafe for them. Explain why privacy (not secrecy) is important. Talk about how their body feels many weird things but they are safe now and we need to care for our bodies so they get better and learn different ways to feel better:

- Do it in your bedroom.
- Wash hands regularly.
- Shower daily as this can become a smelly issue.
- Distraction is great. Using colouring in, knitting or other things to pat and play with can help with sensory stimulation.
- Sex education can be taught regularly and age appropriately.

Managing hygiene provides a sense of being cared for, teaches a child to care for themselves, helps with self-esteem and friendships. Whilst this seems daunting these issues are generally resolved fairly quickly especially with open conversations and predictable routines.

Healthy relationships

Trauma impacts on a child's ability to regulate emotions and control their impulses, trauma also changes the way the child's brain has been established. These factors make it very difficult for children to develop social skills and to understand social cues. Children's behaviour may be over the top when they are excited and becoming very energetic, but this can be scary for other children to experience. A child may become aggressive and violent quickly if things don't go according to plan or if they become triggered, making other children back off. Some children feel nervous and shy which becomes heightened and the child may act out appearing aggressive or stand-offish. These examples make relationships and friendships difficult to create, understand and to maintain.

Social skills are complex and you can use this time to reflect on your own relationships and friendships. As carers we must begin by teaching children how to have healthy friendships and relationships; this is easily role modelled. Empathy plays a big role in friendships, the ability to see something from another's perspective and to understand the feelings of another. An awesome carer that I am blessed to know goes through the rules every morning in the car before school drop off and this helps keep them top of mind and becomes like a bit of a mantra, for example, 'Remember the rules for school, no touching, hands to yourself, see your teacher if you feel uncomfortable and I would like you to make good choices today at school'.

Discuss what the factors are that make a good friend and this includes the child's responsibilities and their rights. Some conversation topics when talking about a new friend might be:

- Is the person safe?
- Someone you can trust?
- Do you enjoy the same things?
- Do you care and support each other?
- Can argue with and have conflict but can make up with them?
- What happens if your friend makes a mistake?
- Can be hurt but can also forgive and expect to be forgiven?
- Not to physical hurt or be physically hurt?
- Makes you laugh and take it in turns when playing together.
- See things from you friend's perspective.
- Discussing self-acceptance and acceptance of others.

Understand that acquiring social skills may take a very long time but each step gets us closer towards being a healthy adult. Even as adults we can come across adult bullies and the better equipped we are to deal with them the better we do and less impact they have on our entire life. Discuss strategies on how to manage and how to cope with big emotions like disappointment and hurt feelings if, for example, a friend plays with someone else. How does jealousy feel and what about just feeling different from others? We must normalise, validate and discuss these emotional responses with our children so they are able to learn.

How do we make relationships?

The four big ones

1. EMPATHY

- Show your child how to read the emotions of other people by looking at their faces, body language and tone of voice. Use movies, books and people watching as practice. This can help develop empathy by discussing how another might be feeling and different perspectives.

- Discuss how emotions feel in our body, what the feeling is and where the feeling is located.

- Get the child engaged at school by being helpful, having small jobs develops responsibility and it always feels good to help out and contribute.

- How to have a conversation — role play asking about their day and guide them to ask about your day. Maybe at dinner everyone can take turns saying 2 good things that happened in their day and 2 not so good things. These examples can be used to discuss social skills relevant to them.

- Name it — 'You seem very *excited* and *energetic* maybe you can go for a jump on the trampoline and have a break from playing.' 'Can you see how I am getting *upset* I want you to stop tugging on my arm.'

- Have a script if you are struggling. You could say, 'Look I am getting upset at the moment I just need some time on my own to calm down. I will get back to you' or 'I am feeling frustrated and tense at the moment. I am going to have some time out in my room for a few minutes I will call you when I come out'.

- Discuss how an uncomfortable feeling in your tummy is generally a warning sign to stay away from this person.

- Plan — write down or discuss and pick out a few people to go to at times of stress.

2. SOCIAL NORMS

- Comment on what social skills the child has and does well.
- Provide opportunities for children to try these skills out and later discuss them. Go out, invite friends over and spend time in different environments such as the library, a show or a movie.
- Work as a team in the home and get teachers onboard.
- Teach a child about compliments, encouragement and praise. Role play giving and receiving compliments.
- Discuss manners and how to say 'please', 'thank you' and 'you're welcome'.
- Saying sorry — what a terrific skill! By guiding a child towards apologising for their unhealthy choices teaches responsibility. You can do this by modelling, saying sorry and saying why you are sorry. This teaches how to repair a relationship as we are not perfect all the time.
- And don't forget hygiene affects friendships.

3. RELATIONSHIP SKILLS

- Teach your child by role playing how to share, borrow and return toys.
- Use dolls, teddy bears or even toy cars to role play social scenarios.
- Teach and encourage eye contact. If looking in the eye is too challenging, try looking at the forehead or between the person's eyes (it is less confronting).
- Share your own experiences with friendships; how you make new friends, how you deal with losing friends, how it feels to you when good friends talk about you behind your back or they make other friends and move on and how you have coped with friendship changes (the good and not so good bits). Everyone goes through this so normalise the experience.
- Find a pen pal or email pal (safety issues, of course) but this is a great way to take time with communication.

4. PROBLEM-SOLVING SKILLS

- Allow choices for the child so they can make decisions.
- Use books and movies to engage the child's attention in understanding how the character works out solutions to problems and complex situations and examples of how the character manages the situation. Show by examples as to what appropriate and inappropriate behaviour is and what is socially acceptable with peers.
- Again teaching problem solving skills with the message that making mistakes is brilliant because everyone does it.
- Teach conflict resolution skills. What do you want to achieve? Break down the steps towards your goal.
- Assertive skills — talk about the difference between assertive, aggressive and passive communication. This can be really fun if role played. Assertive skills are awesome if a child can start practising these early as they help towards healthy personal boundaries.

Learning social skills, social cues and having emotional regulation skills will help a child cope with future problems and will increase healthy decision making, reduce peer pressure, reduce mental health issues such as depression, anxiety, antisocial problems and will increase self-esteem. As we know, life is filled with moments of joy and periods of crappy times, it's random and fluctuates but if children know how to roll with the ups and downs they are more resilient in life, becoming equipped to make goals and plan for future events.

Consequences and planning for healthy changes

Children with traumatic and chaotic backgrounds do not understand cause and effect. Normal strategies such as time out, removal of things like toys and games don't work because they don't understand why their behaviour has led to this happening. These children generally feel rejection, confusion, and will find this similar to how they have been treated before, that things are not permanent so they don't get attached, you will essentially exacerbate behaviour rather than change it.

Children that have trauma backgrounds are sensitive to punishment, generally their past punishment has been confusing, random, possibly violent and unhealthy behaviour may have been encouraged and then next time the same behaviour attracts punishment. However, children must be taught consequences of actions with clear and reasonable boundaries as this encourages healthy relationships.

Let's understand consequences. They should be age appropriate and time limited and never given for a trigger reaction.

- **Natural consequences** are those consequences that are the results of our actions, like to many G&Ts equals a bad headache! Natural consequences for children are THE BEST learning around. For example, we don't wear a jumper to school we get cold, we don't do our homework we get in trouble with the teachers.

- **Logical consequences** are those ones that are given by another. If we speed in our car, we get fined by the police. For children, we or a teacher imposes the consequences for their behaviour, the consequence is related to the behaviour and the child learns responsibility. For example, a child hits another sibling, the logical consequence is we don't hit people and what happens next? You say sorry and do your sister's chores.

Where to start?

What's your bottom line with behaviour? What is not negotiable in the house? These can form house rules. For example, no violence toward any member of the house including animals. Through gentle and age appropriate discussions talk to the child about your expectations of behaviour and what consequences are and how you use them. Even role play with another child or partner make to them laugh. Set some clear rules and the consequences; have these on the fridge so you can point to them. It is so important to be consistent but you also need to be flexible and always have the child calm before attempting to discuss the problem and the consequence that goes with it.

Manage your own feeling of being overwhelmed such as taking yourself to 'time out,' even if you just need to disappear to the loo. The best way is to say, 'I am feeling angry right now so I am going to go into my room for some time out and when I calm down we can talk about what has happened'. If the child continues to escalate with anger you need to address this first, maybe distract them with TV or a cold drink before you leave them.

Children with trauma find it difficult naming what the emotion is they are feeling, and have difficulty with regulating some emotions, especially the big ones. When this happens a child can explode over the smallest thing. For example, ask them to pick up their toys and you could end up with a stuffed penguin heading your way! Best thing to do if it's safe, is to help them get some control over their emotion using breathing exercises, counting, listening to some music, going outside to jump on the trampoline or a swing for a bit. When they are calm talk with them about what is worrying them. You will generally get an answer like 'I don't want to go to school' or 'I have a test tomorrow'. If you don't get an answer try to guess what might be happening, 'Are you worried about going to school tomorrow?'. After a discussion about what they are worried about get them to continue their chores but assure them they are loved and hugged.

Work out a signal with family members or your partner about when to let something go, for example, if a child is determined to wear their socks on their hands while eating dinner. Learn to pick your battles.

'Time in' is a great consequence used for teaching self-regulation in a safe environment, yep, next to you no matter what you are doing. Used for children that are out of control, when they have settled and things are discussed then you can give them a chore to make up for what they have done. Basically you remove them from the unhealthy behaviour and they come and sit beside you whether you are putting clothes on the line or cleaning the bathroom for as long as it takes them to settle. They are not to play or watch TV during this time.

If you have a little person that likes control don't get into a power struggle; let them know you won't engage in the argument and give them a choice on how they want to calm down, for example, 'Sit by me and calm down or sit on the lounge. When you are calm we can talk'.

Some ideas about consequences

- Give them choices — 'What do you think your consequence should be?' I remember working in a youth refuge when I asked the kids this

question the consequence they suggested would generally be more extreme than I would have given them.
- I do love the 5 minutes off your bedtime and as time keeps getting added the behaviour stops. Another great one is doing an extra chore or your sibling's chore (if behaviour was directed at them).
- Have a list of a few consequences on hand when at home or out in public to use.
- Understand that while kids may act out they genuinely may not understand why they are doing this and just need to be helped to calm down.
- Discussions about what happened must occur when the child is completely calm.
- Make a plan for if/when it happens again and give them some ideas on how to approach the situation. If the same behaviour continues maybe look at any potential triggers – what is behind the behaviour.
- Check out what else may be going on. Does the child need food, water, is there a health problem, or are they just tired and emotional and need your attention and nurturing.
- Do not take away any rewards that the child has earnt.

Teachers will welcome a plan with open arms. They will dance a jig and whoop with delight as they won't have to work things out themselves, they will have more understanding for your child and work towards getting results as they have knowledge and strategies.

Let's do a plan that addresses the big ones (see page 113). This is just an example, so make sure you discuss 'the plan' with the teacher and you don't have to go into much detail regarding the child's history except to say they are a kid with trauma and this is what their behaviours are in response to the trauma.

It would be good to meet up with the teacher a few times during the term to check things are working or if there needs to be adjustments. Always make an appointment and give fair warning so the teacher is prepared and can observe the child before the meeting.

Chapter 13   Boundaries and routines — longer term strategies

Sample Consequences Plan

HYGIENE	LYING	STEALING	ACTING OUT
Behaviour Toileting — child tends to not go to the toilet and soils underwear.	**Behaviour** Child will lie about stealing as he is scared of consequence.	**Behaviour** Child will eat all his food at recess and steal at lunch.	**Behaviour** Sexualised behaviour child acts out when excited or stressed. Child will do ....
Plan Teacher will keep extra undies, plastic bag and clothing. Teacher will encourage and remind all children to use toilet. If child is visibly wiggling about send to toilet with another child.	**Plan** Teacher will be given the same script you use for child. Give time until child is ready to discuss and use same consequence but let the child you know what has happened.	**Plan** Teacher will take lunchbox and hand out recess and lunch at appropriate times. Teacher will discuss in circle time not sharing food or taking other's food. If a child is hungry teacher will keep extra food. Parent/carer will provide teacher with enough food for extra snacks during the week.	**Plan** Teacher to place hand on child's shoulder and tell them to wash their hands, give them a squeezy ball to play with or direct the child to another activity. Parent to provide scented hankies for teacher to give to child.
Behaviour Child forgets to wash hands.	**Behaviour** Child will lie and embellish to get attention from peers.	**Behaviour** Child likes to bring pens and things home from peers.	**Behaviour** Child throws things when doesn't get own way.
Plan Teacher to encourage child to wash hands before and after recess and lunch.	**Plan** Teacher to discuss the difference between stories and reality and how it makes other people feel if they know something is not true.	**Plan** Teacher to talk about rules of ownership in class and how each child can help each other sharing and returning. Reward for following the rules.	**Plan** Carer/parent tells teacher the steps to manage this. Time in, then breathing; discuss then consequence which could be to help run a message.

113

Sample scripts for talking about a consequences plan

I can see you are feeling .... come sit by me, do your breathing exercise and then we can talk about it.	I can see that your behaviour is not appropriate for class time. Would you like your squeezy ball/hankie/colouring book?
(When the child is calm) — What happens now?	I know what you have done and I am happy to wait until you are ready to discuss this, you are a great kid and it's okay to make mistakes but we do have to discuss them.
(If child comes up with a consequence that is too much) — Look I think the talk was enough for the moment let's see how we go. Are you happy with that?	When calm — can you tell me what our class rules are regarding hitting others/stealing/lying? Okay so what happens now?

If appropriate talk to the child about the plan that you have with the teacher, not in a way to shame but present it in a way to encourage the child to learn new ways in managing and coping as 'we' all care about you. Get their input on consequences; they may need to help in the canteen at lunch time or help in the library with a friend. Make sure they get praised for the completion of the task. Being in this together lessens the shame and embarrassment.

Chapter 14

Self-esteem

Self-esteem development

Brené Brown (the absolute rockstar of shame research) identifies two types of shame. Normal (for want of a better word) shame that we all have, this shame elicits uncomfortable feelings about our self as a person. Everyday shame encourages correct behaviour and is tied up with our empathy towards others and a desire to be liked and do the right thing. Then there is toxic shame. Toxic shame bubbles away deep down and elicits feelings of worthlessness, self-hatred and, generally, a negative inner belief such as 'I am a bad person'.

Toxic shame is caused by years of childhood abuse and undermines the identity and self-esteem of an individual. For the purposes of this chapter the shame that is referred to here is toxic shame.

While there are several reasons why people have low self-esteem the big one for children from abusive backgrounds is SHAME. Much research has been done about the impact of shame on self-esteem and research (and common sense) suggests that there is not only an association between child abuse and shame but that the impact of shame will influence whether a child

and adult survivor can recover a sense of self-worth. Research tells us that shame impacts a survivor for their entire life.

What is shame? Shame is a crippling emotion that makes the person view themselves as defective, damaged and worthless. Shame produces thoughts in a person that they are incompetent, useless, damaged and unimportant. Then strong emotional reactions such as disgust and anger appear. When a person has this view of themselves they may become avoidant. Behaviours ensure they remain isolated and then this becomes a self-fulfilling prophecy, reducing the experience for people to have proper healthy relationships which further exacerbates low self-esteem.

Self-esteem is the keystone to mental health, good relationships, healthy personal boundaries, success and confidence. One thing to know is when self-esteem increases behaviours change which is a good guideline to keep in mind, but how do we start building this?

A healthy lifestyle which includes adequate sleep, a healthy diet, regular exercise (yep, sport) and a safe environment will support the development of a healthy self-esteem and the development of social skills and social interaction. You could come up with a groovy diagram that has loads of arrows to show that when basic needs are met there is an increase in healing of all these lovely brain and emotional parts in a child.

Here's a list of the hows:

- A safe and nurturing home (who would have thunk it).
- Regular validation of the child's thoughts and feelings as well as teaching feelings that go with thoughts and situations.
- Teach self-acceptance by giving examples of how everyone in the world is different and has different backgrounds, talk about the statistics (well, don't get the whiteboard and a calculator out) but talk about how many kids have experienced what they have and that's why they write books like this, have many, many foster care agencies, etc.
- If appropriate meet up with other carers and children in foster care.
- Teach self-efficacy by giving the child small tasks, encouraging and praising and then move on to more complex tasks.
- Teach problem solving skills by talking about how you go about solving problems and approaching tasks (even little ones) and make sure you involve the child by asking their advice. Break things down into simple, small tasks and reward each success.
- Talk about planning, forward thinking (what will happen next if you do that) and consequences of those choices. Consequences are not necessarily negative.

- Discuss and talk about making goals, keep it small to begin with. For example, your goal for the week can be if you have a shower each night you get to choose a movie to watch on Friday night.

- Give some control around making decisions, healthy choices and praising the success. If a failure occurs talk it through and remember we all make mistakes. Mistakes are necessary for growth.

- Part of learning to manage success and to achieve goals is to ask for help. Teach the child how to ask for help — through language and action. For example, if at school put your hand up, say excuse me and speak out your request. This can be scary for a child as they may have never been helped before and independence is for them strength- or fear-based. Let the child know they are a rockstar when it comes to asking for help, the first time is the hardest and the more they practice and get good results the more these building blocks will increase self-worth and confidence.

- Be open and available to talk about their past experiences and normalise their feelings and reactions. Tell them if this happened to you how you would feel. Don't shut them down when they speak even if you feel uncomfortable, this is the child's experience and needs to be validated. This will lead to attachment and help to process the trauma.

- Language is so important when trying to reduce the impact of internalised shame so don't 'guilt-trip', don't tease the child about personal things, or put down the child even it seems harmless. Be playful but mindful. Drop words like 'should', 'ought' and change 'why' to 'what' or 'how'. Also drop 'good girl' and 'good boy' out of language if you can as this can be a real trigger for some children. Simply use 'thank you' or 'that's right', 'well done', 'great work'.

- Remember you are always the model to your child so tell them how you feel and how you are going to manage your emotion. You can ask for their advice too. 'I am feeling disappointed, sad, hurt and/or angry because Netflix removed my favourite show (or another valid reason — age appropriate obviously) so I may have to go for a walk outside (the 'how' of managing this emotion), what do you think I could do?

- Validate the negative emotions because we all have them. It's okay to be angry, jealous, sad, and cranky.

- Add 'enough' — you are good enough, you are smart enough, you are brave enough, you are happy enough, and kind enough. Try and get away from comparing your child to others and help them not to compare themselves to others but stress how unique they are and how important they are to you and the family.

- Have discussions about what it means to be unique. Encourage a child's interests no matter how diverse they are. Allow your child to get muddy, play outside, catch tadpoles, walk in the rain, run around the oval with a dog, kick leaves — there is always a nice warm shower after a playful day.

- Encourage your child to express themselves by trying out a drama class, an art class, singing or music. This will help develop confidence, gives a child feedback and encouragement, and supports self-expression in a nonconfrontational way but one that will be heard.

- Find out what they like and teach them to make personal judgments on things such as if they like hot chocolates or milkshakes more and what are the reasons. What sort of TV shows make them feel good and engages them. Developing personal judgments and tastes in a variety of areas is important for self-knowledge.

- Teach positive self-talk especially after making a bad choice. You can even use movies as examples of how characters change their self-talk. The first step is to notice the negative talk, what is it? Practice countering the negatives with positives. Maybe developing some scripts would be helpful.

- Teach the child to turn their disappointment into opportunity — this is reframing and it is really good to be able to understand this concept early. If the child is disappointed that they have to miss out on a play date with a friend because they have to go to a family barbecue then they can use that event as a topic of conversation when they next catchup with their friend.

- Use imagination with the child through imagining successful situations.

- Play Uno — I know right….whaat! It actually builds executive functioning. It teaches a child how to take turns, to think strategy, teaches winning and losing, and teaches planning skills while developing motor skills. When Uno is going well move up in complexity to easy through more advanced board games. BUT not video games!

- Challenge shame and face fear. Teach the child to pause and focus and to ask 'is this really scary or is it my imagination'.

- Discuss how to take risks and what will happen if they succeed or fail. Stress that it is okay either way. Examples are asking a peer to come over for a play afternoon, trying out an activity or new food. Age appropriate stress is okay for kids but remember these children are coming with high levels of stress so make these risks small and monitor them.

- Help develop personal safety skills whilst validating the child by stressing that they were able to manage abuse and now they can learn other skills to help keep them safe. Never, ever ask a child why they didn't tell anyone about what was happening.

- Teaching social skills, such as how to have conversations, how to read social cues all help to encourage friendships. Teaching a child assertive communications skills help develop healthy relationships and healthy personal boundaries.

- Discuss what healthy and unhealthy friendships are. How do we know if our friend is not healthy — what do we feel in our body? Most kids do feel some sort of discomfort around another individual who is not healthy for them.

- Teach the art of giving and receiving a compliment. This builds empathy as the child is looking for what they believe to be a positive trait that they can compliment a person on. Receiving a compliment and replying 'thank you' produces self-worth and gets a child physically responsive to positive reinforcement.

- Being able to manage conflict is an essential tool for healthy self-esteem. Talking about why conflicts arise and when fights and arguments occur that it is important to repair and make up so that it is not a major impact on the child's life.

- It is also important to teach the 'smile and wave' technique. So after a good old barny with a friend and the child does not want to continue the friendship, teach them how to be pleasant, friendly and respectful but they still have the choice not to continue the friendship.

And then there is the matter of rights and responsibilities. We all have rights — the right to a safe home, the right to have our basic needs met, etc. But we also have responsibilities; so we have the right to be safe at school and we have the responsibility to behave in safe ways and follow instruction. Your child may have had their human rights violated so why would they need to be responsible or even have any understanding of the concept. The easiest way to encourage this learning and development is through communication and reminding the child and also having a pet. Learning to be responsible for a puppy or any other type of pet, by taking care of and being responsible for another allows this area of the child's development to thrive. Obviously, an age-appropriate pet and one you can manage as the child will need support.

Identity and culture

Identity, hey, how do you explain that? Simply put, it is your physical, emotional, spiritual and intellectual being. Identity is a mish-mash of who you are, what you like, what you dislike, what you value, what you agree and disagree with, what you find disgusting or heart-warming, what makes you comfortable and uncomfortable, how you deal with things, your interests, what you find funny, your personality, what you look like, what your history and family influences are.

Self-esteem is closely related to identity and having a healthy and stable foundation and sense of who you are and where you come from supports a good self-esteem, self-acceptance and promotes good mental health. Having a strong sense of self and a healthy self-esteem encourages healthy choices, healthy relationships and positive behaviour.

Your self-esteem begins to develop as a small child. If a child becomes distressed and is nurtured and encouraged then the child believes and feels they are important and valuable. Children with complex trauma have very little experience with being nurtured, safe and cared for; they begin life with a sense of not being important or valued. Self-esteem and identity continues to develop throughout our life. Imagine the impact on a child that has a history of severe neglect. This child begins school feeling pretty bad and different from other children. This child may be smelly, unkempt and hungry, begging or stealing food. Other children refuse to play with this child and teachers may not notice or intervene for this child. The child's sense of worthlessness is reinforced which negatively impacts on self-esteem and identity. OMG, this happens to little kids!

Unfortunately we as loving carers can't change the way children feel about themselves even by hanging off the light fittings and screaming out how incredibly wonderful they are, nor can we wave a magic wand to change

Chapter 14   Self-esteem

the bad experiences. What we can do is provide the child with a safe and nurturing environment so they can become themselves. Stand back and guide them gently in positive ways. Know this will take a long time, years in fact, this is ongoing as these little people's brains are wired with survival. To develop this brain we need to go back to the beginning as well as teaching them to think critically.

Ask them what they think about things, talk to them about current issues, play board games, talk to your partner about what is going on in the world in front of them (age appropriate) and normalise input especially from the media. TV shows portray happy families that are loving and supportive but in the real world this is not always the case.

Culture

A bit about culture. What is it? It is where you come from, what your people believe, what your ancestry is, and what your family of origin's beliefs and rituals are through language used, daily tasks, stories told and history.

The catchword for carers is having 'cultural competence' and whilst it sounds like the result you get from taking an important test, cultural competence is really about being open to learning about your child's background and where they come from, whether it is from the next town or from a culturally diverse background. The message is to be curious, encouraging and supportive. This is a little human that has a history that may be different to your own; be aware of your own judgments, beliefs and prepare to have some of your own beliefs challenged, maybe not, but prepare anyway.

While you may dash to the library to borrow every book written on a specific culture just remember that there are many differences within a culture. Certainly do some research and get some knowledge but getting to know and understand your child is the best way to gain information and understanding about their experience.

What is your important responsibility is to teach a child how to manage racism and discrimination if ever confronted by this, in such a way that they feel no shame. Give examples of how some people learn to be racist and mean, and some people are scared and this makes them angry. Look at how many different people are in the world. Teach the child pride and acceptance of themselves and others.

Ahaa! Celebrations I hear you ask. If you come from a fairly typical Anglo background you would probably celebrate Christmas and Easter and more than likely have seen a bit in the media around arguments and viewpoints on Christmas and Easter celebrations. I am of the belief that if you come from an Easter bunny-loving, Santa-hugging background you should continue on with this as this is your tradition. However, discussions with the child about how you and your family celebrate as well as incorporating the child's celebrations into your own can be helpful. This also applies to children going into an alternate culture. It is imperative that their own traditions are considered and continued.

Including culturally specific and family rituals into daily life may freak out with all the other things to manage and think about. How can you possibly do this as well! Sorry to be slightly confronting but frankly it is your responsibility to do this; it is not just important to include these aspects into your parenting, it is essential. Yep, I get it there are times this is difficult to get your head around — parenting from your own background with the inclusion of additional cultural factors. Most people are so worried about getting it wrong and offending but please don't be. Remember to be humorous — simply trying will enrich the child's life. Think it's hard for you. Try being the child from another culture and attempting to fit in to your culture — learn together.

Hound the caseworker for ideas and information. It is their job to have a cultural plan that outlines how to do this or what is expected. Jump up and down if need be to make sure you have a cultural plan as this is essential for the child's identity and wellbeing.

The 'how' of culture and birth family rituals

- Be curious in a non-confrontational way. So no questioning and probing just gentle interest.

- Understand that culture and identity is not just about skin colour or where the child was born. Your child is an interesting human being with a story and a history so find out about it to help them explore.

- Learn some language such as certain words or phrases (also share with the child's teacher).

- Cook and serve culturally specific food or food that was important to the child and keeps a birth family connection.

- Get information from the library or internet, find culturally specific events to attend, and community events. One of the best ways is to ask the child's caseworker, buy books, DVDs, YouTube, art/craft and toys.

- It is very important to understand your own cultural identity including language, traditions and rituals, handed down stories, your ancestors and your own history, and by teaching the child your cultural heritage over time and learning about theirs encourages a sense of belonging, identity and self-esteem.

- Print off colouring-in pictures or research craft activities.
- If possible find friends from the same background or just encourage joining in with a group or activity.

Identity

- Discuss and talk about values as these shape identity, such as being honest, being a good friend, being trustworthy, being respectful and being respected, being responsible, trying the best you can, making mistakes and learning from them and having compassion for yourself and others.
- Sport and more sport. Have I mentioned this? Research says those engaged in sport have a higher self-esteem, do better academically, are more motivated and positive, and are able to manage anxiety and depression better.
- Helping others is a very important factor in forming identity and healthy self-esteem as this gesture is a way of feeling good about oneself and comes from a place of compassion towards others. Providing opportunities to be helpful such as playing with the neighbour's dog, doing chores, helping teachers or grandparents and being rewarded with praise.
- Special occasions such as birthdays and Christmas may well increase a child's anxiety. Start off with low key, calm events introducing the child slowly to your celebrations. Try and aim for calm and predictable, prepare the child by lots of discussions of what to expect at the celebration and give them a safe place to go if needed. Don't put out 1001 presents for their 6th birthday and invite all your relatives, friends, neighbours, and the local fire brigade (though I can see the importance of this just in case!) to an afternoon party which may be a tad overwhelming.
- Put up photos and pictures, displaying these next to those of your own birth family. Be inclusive.

Chapter 14   Self-esteem

- Develop rituals and traditions together as a new family system. Introduce them slowly and only introduce those that you are able to continue with. If you decide to do an Easter egg hunt with hundreds of clues hidden all over the house, backyard and local neighbourhood — be prepared to do this every year forever!
- Simple is good with rituals.
- Be curious and find out what things your child likes, give choices and ask 'what do you like about that choice?'
- Music is great to have playing in the background to increase a child's awareness and movement plus it's a great mood enhancer.

- Meet as many people in their family as you are able to, past teachers and friends if any and try and support the continuation of these relationships even if only via email as long as you supervise (definitely no Instagram, Snapchat, Kick, Facebook etc.). I worked with one family where this girl loved her elderly neighbours as they used to look after her at times, we tracked them down and she visited them. This was so important to her and it was able to validate some memories and events for her plus it gave her something positive to take from her experience. Another young boy spoke of a teacher at a previous school who used to keep clean uniforms, underwear, and deodorant at school; he would change when he got to school and before he went home change back into his other clothes. This boy thought this was amazing and continues to email this teacher.
- Consistently work together to develop and add to life story work.

As a carer you should also inform the school of any culturally significant practices or expectations so that the teachers have a better understanding of the child's upbringing and are then able to better support the child. Teachers are so fab when it comes to student inclusion practices as they have so many ideas to be able to make special events for all the kids in the class to learn about specific cultures.

Life story work

Life story work is the written information of a child's time within out of home care whether this is with foster parents, adoptive parents or extended family members. Life story work is usually kept in a chronological timeline of where a child has lived, the schools they have attended and some poignant events that have occurred. This is all very, let's say, clinical and structured and life is definitely not like that.

Sadly, some agencies are not very forthcoming with a child's more detailed history due to privacy reasons and large gaps in the child's life may exist. It would be helpful to a carer if they are aware of some of the more significant issues in a child's life so they can have some understanding of potential triggers, potential conversations, and to validate a child's experience. Mostly abuse happens in secrecy so by keeping this abuse history secret from the carer keeps the narrative going and the feelings of shame and worthlessness alive within the child. Having an understanding of the child's life allows the carer to support the development of the child's narrative, their story, which includes the good bits and the not so good bits.

Life story books are usually provided by the agency and have ideas and instructions on how to complete and add to them but you can make your own and the child is encouraged to participate during the process. By learning about the child's history and understanding their past also allows understanding of their behaviours and gives the child a witness without judgement which supports a healthy identity.

Children are able to look back over their books and discuss their experiences with their carer and this can be helpful with memory and awareness. Memory and a life narrative can prevent the child from romanticising why they are in care and supports their understanding of their life which again helps with acceptance and validation. Life story work helps provide the space for children to ask difficult questions such as why can't my parents look after me, why am I in care and so forth.

What do you include in a life story record? Basically a life story book is a written timeline and history of the child's life and experiences from birth to the present day. Most information you may receive from the agency but extra things may include:

- A genogram (family tree).
- Spiritual and cultural information such as were they named after anyone in particular, some words in their language, what are the significant beliefs and meaning behind these.
- Life story records culture, religion and family rituals such as special words and memories that may be lost as the child grows.
- Photos (school photos, photos from daily events or even things they like, most people have smartphones these day so snapping off a few isn't time-consuming).
- Photos of parents, previous carers, pets, old and new friends make their life big.
- School information such as reports, awards, photos of things that occur at school.
- Artwork including drawings, obviously you can't put a huge chunk of clay into the book but you can take a photo of their creations.

- Cards, letter, mementos from parents or previous carers. If you can't fit it in take a photo.

- Include details of previous placements, use a map or Google Earth to add so the child has a point of reference, also schools and friendship groups or activities they were involved in.

- As we know, the child's life may be full of loss and unhappy events and we do have to add these in but we do it in a way that is appropriate. If a parent has been a sexually abusive I wouldn't add in a picture and description of the parent as this may not be appropriate to include but you could put in an image that the child chooses to represent this person. Caseworkers are really helpful for providing this information.

- Most carers will have a folder or book and a box to keep favourite toys, favourite clothes, and bits and pieces. Kids love going through this stuff as they get older.

- Keep these things safe so they can't get to them. Believe me, if they are emotionally overwhelmed and it is in sight it will be destroyed.

Let's move on to another type of life story work. A fella in the United Kingdom called Richard Rose, is the author of *Life Story Therapy: A new therapy for traumatised children.* He has done some very good podcasts. He works with carers and children to develop attachment and connection through the sharing of both parties' life stories. This enables the carer to truly understand what the child has experienced and how they behave in certain ways and to also reflect on their own upbringing, again understanding where they come from. Richard suggests that this is very powerful as it increases awareness, understanding, compassion, empathy, trust and, most of all, attachment between carer and child.

Another top bloke is John Briere (yet another king of trauma treatment), who uses life story therapy to treat trauma by allowing the carer and the child to openly discuss their history in a safe way, to support any grief and loss, and develop attachment through the PACE principles (see Chapter 7) which enhances a child's identity and cultural connection.

By working with life story a carer is able to be self-reflective and understand their own history and the impact of this on their own development, values and identity and sharing this with the child whilst understanding the child's own behaviours and history. Life story work can be a springboard to take this work deeper. For example if you are working on a period of the child's life when they went to a certain school. Find out about the good and bad experiences and share your own bullying or bad experiences and how you survived them.

Remember to start small, find out as much information as possible about the child and begin to have conversations. Using the life story book is the start of learning about your child and to support the development of identity and self-acceptance.

SECTION 4

Looking After Yourself

Chapter 15

Care for carers

Staying sane — strategies for self-care

On our quest to support and care for a child with complex trauma and meeting challenges with love and humour we may actually lose ourselves in this journey. What I am getting at is that while you are providing a loving, nurturing and safe home and life for your child who is caring for you?

I am going to be quite honest here because you need to get this from the outset you are not going to get much back from these children except to see small changes in behaviour and small miracles along the way. The absolute message I really want you to take from this is that everyone, all of us make mistakes, we all mess up and we all say things that we might later regret. But the most important part of messing up is the repair we make after and that means take responsibility for your error, apologise and explain without blame, 'Sorry I raised my voice, I was very tired and it was the wrong thing but I can't promise that I never will because I might make a mistake again. I love you and it's not your fault'.

Adult relationships are a little more complex with some people not allowing you the space to repair the mess-up and other people who you decide are not healthy to have in your life. This is something you can use to discuss with the children as to how some friends come and go in life, that you may miss things about them but other aspects of the friendship may not be good to have around. We all know how awful the double-edged apology is, 'I am sorry but if you didn't do ... then I wouldn't have done ...', or the minimiser, 'Well, I did the wrong thing but it wasn't that bad, I don't know why you are carrying on so much.' Blame and shame has no space in a child's life. Validate the child's experience, have empathy and help to heal their feelings, it's not rocket science!

Have you heard about the analogy regarding the airplane? It goes something like this:

> If you were sitting on a plane with your family and there was an emergency that made the oxygen masks fall out of the ceiling. What the flight attendants tell you to do is firstly place the oxygen mask on yourself before you attend to your child. Why you ask? Well if you don't you will probably die and then your whole family would die from lack of oxygen as everyone would be panicking. If you attend to yourself first then you have a better chance of getting the masks onto your kids so everyone lives, yay! Unless you crash. The moral of the story? Put yourself first, care for yourself first, your needs first and only then you can help others.

I remember someone wise saying that you must always be responsible for yourself first. When you do this you have the energy and mental health to be responsible for your relationship and partner, and if the relationship is healthy and strong then you are able to be responsible for your children who will reap the benefits of having a safe, healthy parent/carer/family to grow up in. If you are not in a relationship you must be responsible for yourself and ensure you have super friends or family members to support you, or if you and your partner choose to separate, be responsible for the healthy outcome of the separation.

What's burnout? Burnout is when you have experienced overwhelming levels of stress for a lengthy period of time. Burnout causes emotional and physical exhaustion which can lead to high levels of anguish, loss of memory and ability to focus, lack of motivation, anxiety and depression. When you are caring for a child with complex needs you may feel overwhelmed, exhausted, lonely and drained. One of the indicators of burnout is a lack of social support — ringing any bells? What is the cue for preventing burnout — simple — self-care. Being responsible for your needs first and foremost. If you do this you will have more energy, more support and better mental health. You deserve it!

The business of self-care

Break self-care down into daily, weekly, monthly and long-term activities.

- *Daily* — whether it's the morning, during the day or evening give yourself 1 hour of uninterrupted 'me time'.
- *Weekly* — take some space (for a coffee or a wine with a friend or, god forbid, don your activewear and get out there for a walk), whatever it is you have to do, do it weekly and for a few hours. Make it a routine, give yourself something to look forward to.
- *Monthly* — take a mental health day, head off shopping, go to the gym, see a movie, give it to yourself to look forward to your day.
- Baths — candles, books and ban interruptions.
- Read a book or join or start a book club. A long-term foster carer (another I am blessed to know) has started an online book club with other carers where they talk about a book and check in with each other to make sure everyone is doing okay.
- Talk to others about fostering a child.
- Oh, and here is the big one — see a counsellor, you may need to debrief or maybe just to keep sane (crying and hitting your head several times against a wall might not be the best answer!). This is really hard work. Seeing a counsellor can help monitor your stress levels and prevent burnout and also provide you with support and suggestions for strategies.
- Remember when you have a child in care you may lose friends, your social life and acquaintances may change and you may make new friends. Continue to catch up with your friends even with phone calls or a quick coffee. Stay connected.
- Get yourself a hobby, one you can pick up as needed, such as knitting, painting, roller derby, kick-boxing, gardening.
- Leave the house to engage in the world. Go swimming, bushwalking or just out to lunch and make this regular.

- What about getting your hair or nails done, massage, or facial regularly.
- Write yourself a list and keep adding daily, short-term and long-term self-care strategies and goals to it.
- Burn aromatherapy oils.
- Listen to music.
- Parent time and, make sure it happens. You both need to ensure your relationship is healthy.
- Date nights, yes, we have all heard about them but many couples don't follow up because it gets too hard, things come up or it is put it off. You must make this a priority Set a time each month and guard it with your life!
- Understand your own anxiety reaction. Are you into fight, flight or freeze? What's your background? What are your triggers?
- You have a responsibility to address your own trauma issues, whether it is childhood trauma, being bullied at school or being excluded from a social group because I will guarantee that this will be triggered throughout your caring for a vulnerable child.
- Have a list of safe people you can call on when you are at your wits' end and need a break. It could be a neighbour, a friend or a relative.
- Holidays —Yay!
- Celebrate the small miracles, they do happen.

What about respite care?

Family and Community Services NSW define respite care as 'planned, regular or one-off time-limited breaks for foster carers'. Respite care is also available for adoptive parents and kinship carers. Respite care is when a child has time with another approved family to give some time-out for their carer.

Some carers feel that respite care is a sign that they are a failure or unable to cope, and don't want to consider this as it is a negative reflection on their parenting capacity. Well, dear carer, it is precisely the opposite! Respite is

self-care and important to the health of your relationship. Remember date night? This is how you make it happen and, guess what, you become a more relaxed and calmer carer.

Respite carers are approved caregivers that (if you are truly lucky) can become regular respite carers for you child, just like a babysitter or your own family members. This gives you a sense of relationship to them and it also encourages your child to form healthy relationships with other families.

Respite care can be provided in your own home or in another family's home for a few hours, a day, a weekend or even some time over the school holidays. If respite occurs in another's home make sure the child meets the family first and spends some time with you there, transition is where children have big issues. Always allow the child to have some of their own things to take such as a toy or blanket, even a calendar or clock they can mark time with and make sure you are available on the phone.

Does respite impact on attachment? Personally, I think it depends on the child. Some kids love going to their respite carer's home and then coming home is a little exciting. You know when you go on holiday, have a great time but when you get back and walk in the door it's lovely to be home. Same goes for kids, back in their room, their family, smells become familiar etc. While some kids hate it and become anxious and withdrawn, you will need to make the preparation longer and come from a more therapeutic transition for these children to adapt. Never use respite as a punishment as you will just be setting up the placement for failure.

School holiday camps are offered to children in care and most of these are fantastic, have great activities, are safe and an opportunity to meet other children. However, let's talk about the impact of going to a camp on your child. Mostly camps are attended by other children in similar situations so that has good and bad consequences; I guess you need to be mindful of how this camp serves your child. Would you send your own child away to these camps every school holiday? When a child in care is sent to camp and a birth child stays at home this can create huge issues of rejection, feelings of being outside the family, may impact on the child's self-worth and they may feel punished. This is a tricky balance as your birth children certainly deserve some time alone with their parents. What can be helpful is getting the child involved in the decisions, give the child some ideas and find out what they would like to do, obviously you have to make the decisions but talking about this gives you time to evaluate their emotional state. Instead of school holiday camps try other alternatives such as a safe relative carer either on your side or one of their family members and always talk to the caseworker about other options.

Vicarious trauma

The term *vicarious trauma* was developed by Lisa McCann and Laurie Anne Pearlman in the early 1990s (what amazing women to come up with this concept). Vicarious trauma is described as one person experiencing in their imagination through actual feelings what has occurred in another's life, mainly the trauma they have experienced. There has been research that suggests that a person who works with people with PTSD can actually develop symptoms of PTSD themselves. While most research was centred on workers in trauma fields and the slow build-up or the cumulative effect of vicarious trauma it is also important to consider yourself and your family members.

The impact on the family when caring for a child that has complex trauma can be significant and as time goes on, bonds form, attachment is made and feelings of devastation and grief for what this child went through can be overwhelming.

Some of the warning signs:

- Symptoms of anxiety and depression.
- Feeling overwhelmed by strong emotions such as anger, fear, sadness, grief and despair.
- Intrusive traumatic thoughts, dreams, nightmares or flashbacks.
- Lack of motivation and energy (different to your current level).
- Increased cynicism and lack of humour.
- Increased thought of life being unfair and a lack of social justice.
- Increased sense of the world being dangerous and a lack of trust in people.
- Problems with your own intimate relationships, feelings of being alone and feeling helpless to change things.
- Sleeping problems.
- Can't handle any type of violence on TV.
- Increased medication or substance use.
- Preoccupation with what experiences another person has had.

How do you prevent vicarious trauma, burnout and high stress levels? Self-care! This is also where having your own counsellor is helpful as they are outside your network and can keep an eye on you and offer their professional support. Most trauma workers have professional supervision to help them manage the work they do, the stories they hear and the feelings they have in response to this work. Carers live with these traumatised children and experience their behaviour, their trauma reactions, their triggers, their overwhelming emotion and anguish and the child's grief — and you don't get to go home after work. This is why it is ESSENTIAL that you practise SELF-CARE!

What happens if you can't do it anymore?

The reality is that caring for a child with complex trauma is hard work, rewarding but emotionally and physically draining at times. A child comes to you with a background of despair and abuse — basically their human rights have been violated. This is not their fault and as a carer you must be able to see the behaviour as a result of trauma not that the child is being naughty. Most carers give children the most amazing experiences; they provide love and safety a nurturing environment and attend to every one of their needs and still things sometimes don't work out. If you decide that you can't care for the child anymore do not blame yourself (I know you will), seek professional counselling to work through your decision and grief reactions. You are not a bad person for doing this, in fact, you are strong and wonderful to know that you and your family (remember self-care) are not the right family for this child. In making this decision you will do a number of things.

- You are making an informed decision about whether the placement can continue.
- You are role modelling to your own children that self-care is important and that they are important.
- You have given your all to this child and are being responsible for their needs.
- You are allowing the child the opportunity to have a more suitable home based on the child's needs.
- During the time that the child has lived with you, you have been able to provide a loving, safe and nurturing home giving the child an experience and evidence that this exists.
- You are able to continue contact on a more informal basis with the child and/or offer respite to new carers, if you and the caseworker feel this is appropriate.

A bit about biological children

You must take into account your children's thoughts and feelings because adapting to new family structures is difficult. I recommend that as a family you talk about the 'bottom line'. This is where you decide to 'call it' and have a break from caring. This can be if the child in care displays sexualised behaviour that does not reduce but puts family members at risk, physical assaults that impact on your children. Go through a checklist with each member of the family to ascertain mental health, such as lack of sleep, intrusive thoughts, anxiety, depression and withdrawal. Have a plan, be prepared and this will be your safety net.

Biological children often get overlooked when it comes to attention, and this is definitely no ones' fault, it is just that traumatised children require much more attention and supervision. Biological children may also be exposed to the emotional and behavioural responses from the child and this can be highly traumatising to witness. This can be difficult for adults and our children don't, as yet, have the skills needed to understand triggers and reactions.

Some biological children can become overwhelmed, fearful, anxious and stressed and this can turn to feeling resentment and jealousy towards the traumatised child. Some parents can put extra pressure on biological children to do extra household chores, achieve better at school and, without realising, push them into independence before they are possibly ready. The impact may be that biological children become withdrawn and, in some cases, act out and put themselves at risk.

Probably the best idea is to read some of the research available and talk to caseworkers about the impact on your own children prior to making any decisions so you know what to look out for.

How do you support your children?

- Be open and honest (again age appropriately).
- Celebrate wins and verbalise them.

- Include the biological children in all decisions.
- Have a 'bottom-line exit plan'.
- Encourage biological children to be involved in their own activities — and, yep, sport is the best!
- Encourage biological children to have their own outlet and friendship groups.
- Notice them and spend one-on-one time with them each week to check in with them and to be present.
- If there is a support group around for biological children encourage your child to join it.
- If needed, have a counsellor for your child to off-load to. This will also ensure someone is keeping an eye on their mental health plus it gives them someone to talk to who is not in their social circle.

- Teach biological children self-care strategies and make these as important as your own.

Please don't get me wrong here, caring for a child with complex trauma can be so absolutely wonderful and rewarding but you need to fully understand how adding another family member will impact on your current family. It is also important that you are able to meet the needs of these complex little people and to have as much support for you and your family as this will ensure the family is healthy.

SECTION 5

Further Support

Chapter 16

Tools of the trade

Let's acknowledge that caring for a child with complex trauma is difficult and the more tools we have up our sleeves the better, and let's also acknowledge that at times we will forget we have these tools at our disposal and would prefer to hide under our doonas ploughing through a box of chocolates while watching *Netflix* (well, this is my idea of self-care). My thoughts are to jot down a few simple tools, trial them and either keep them or scrap them. Sometimes things work really well and then overnight they don't so it's good to mix up strategies and try new things but also to notice the miracles as this keeps you hopeful.

Attack things in order of priority. Think about what is the biggest issue that is presenting and begin there. Pick three strategies per issue and play around with these. I know it's pretty overwhelming when you see all the strategies and all the issues that you may be confronted with. Take it slowly and one step at a time. And, remember, always think of the five big ones.

1. Don't take it personally.
2. Use humour.
3. Try something new.
4. Breathe and notice the stress in your body.
5. Know that it's one step forward, three steps back.

You have many strategies to use plus you have access to a bunch of professionals and the internet for more strategies and support — use them.

When we become overwhelmed we can sometimes forget things so having a notebook to jot down ideas can be helpful especially as a record for your own purposes.

Here's an idea of how you might list these:

Date	Behaviour	Strategy	Work or not?
No idea haven't slept for a month. Think we are in 2020.	Luke can't settle at night, won't sleep more than 2 hours at a time and has nightmares.	Putting house to sleep	Works half the time.
		Paediatrician — trial melatonin and magnesium.	Seems to be helping. No
		Oils and books	Yes so far.
		Meditation CDs	(since taking meds easier to go to sleep but still waking, CD helps through the night to put back to sleep).

Here are some ideas that can help distract the child from challenging behaviours and help them to calm themselves.

Sorting tray

Sorting trays are great way for mindful activities. Mix up the activities and have about 5 on a tray at a time. Montessori classrooms have awesome ideas for the development of fine motor skills they incorporate in activities. You will need to hit your local reject shop or craft shop and you will need a tray, a bunch of little boxes or containers and craft items.

Here is a list to start with:

- Small container with holes in top, use colourful toothpicks (from a $2 shop) and the child inserts these in to the holes.

- Different coloured little pom poms to separate in to colours. Use little boxes.
- Stickers to stick on a piece of paper.
- A mix of shells to sort through and separate in to sizes or colours.
- Beads and buttons, again, sorting in to piles or little boxes.
- Taking stamps off envelopes.
- Felt shapes sorted in to similar shapes.
- Pack of playing cards sorted in to numbers or suits.
- Pictures of animals sorted and grouped (you can buy cards of animals).
- Kids like playing with Pokémon.
- Coloured pencils or crayons to sort out in piles.
- Scrap material or felt pieces.
- Small toys such as tiny cars or dolls like shopikan stuff.
- Sort Lego pieces in to colours.
- Nuts and bolts to be put together or taken apart.

Other sorting ideas include:

- Some children love to play in and sort out Tupperware drawers.
- Teach your child to fold socks and tea towels.
- Sort out tool boxes.
- Sort out CDs and books.

'Go-To' box

Definitely not a new idea but one that works really well for children. The idea is to have a small box like a shoebox or something of similar size. Have some fun with your child decorating it and then you put things into the box that can help distract the child, help them calm down and this becomes a mindful stress reducing activity. Because of the size of the box you can take it anywhere. Just keep changing the items in the box, not when the child is bored but at regular intervals as you actually don't want the child to become bored with the box it needs to be a 'Go To' at times of overwhelm.

What goes in the box?

- Small toys, just a few, cars, shopikans.
- Squeezy ball.
- Slime or playdough.
- Snow domes.
- Sugar-free lollypop.
- Stickers and paper.
- A small kaleidoscope.
- Container of shiny stars.
- Container of pom poms.
- Container of buttons.
- Bubbles to blow.
- Stuffed toy.
- Hankie with aromatherapy oil on it.
- A balloon to blow up.
- Feathers (you can blow them up in the air and try and keep them up by blowing on them, or tickling your arms or face with them).
- Colouring book and pencils.
- iPod and headphones with music or a story.
- Fidget spinners.
- Rubik's cube.
- Bendy toys.

Check out Pinterest for more ideas. Water play is great too. Give the child a sink or a big plastic container with water and some little containers, shells, plastic toys or any suitable fiddly things to play with in the water.

A little bit of cognitive–behaviour therapy

Teaching a child how their mind works is really difficult so the following is an example of how you can begin teaching them the relationship between thoughts, feelings and behaviour and how replacing negative thoughts with positive thoughts will help the child develop better control over their emotions and build resilience. Here are two examples.

Example 1: The child steals money from their carer and gets in trouble.

Negative Thought	Feeling	Behaviour
My Mum hates me.	Sad	Lie
I am bad and naughty.	Frightened	Break my toys.
I don't care.	Angry	Hide under my bed.
	Lonely	Yell and cry.
Positive Thought	**Feeling**	**Behaviour**
I did the wrong thing but I can talk about it with Mum.	Anxious and sa.	Sit and listen to Mum.
	Bad	Do my consequence.
I may get in trouble but I won't get hurt and she won't make me leave.		Understand that it's just a blip and I will try not to do it next time.

Example 2: The child's friend does not play with them at school.

Negative Thought	Feeling	Behaviour
My friend doesn't like me.	Sad	Yell at my friend.
I am not good enough.	Angry	Cry and get angry.
I am a bad friend.	Lonely	Be violent.
Positive Thought	**Feeling**	**Behaviour**
Even though I am hurt and sad my friend can play with other kids.	Anxious and sad.	Ask for help.
	Calm.	Find another friend.
I can ask the teacher to help me find another friend.		Have fun.
		Not get in more trouble.
I can go to the library.		

Breathing exercises

There are many fantastic websites and practitioners out there that can teach these. All breathing exercises are aimed at being slow and controlled. Here are a few you might like to try with your child. You can also use them yourself when taking a little time for self-care.

- Put your hands on your belly and while you are breathing in try and blow up your belly with your breath.
- Breathe in to the count of 3 and out to the count of 3. Then try and extend to the count of 6.
- Smell the flowers and blow out the candles — slow breath in and a big breath out.
- Draw a box with your breath and make it bigger (so breathe in while you imagine drawing the side of the box with your breath, breathe out as you go across the top, in as you go down the other side and out as you go across the bottom making a box).
- This is really cool and works — put your tongue really firmly behind your top teeth while you breathe in and then drop your tongue to behind your bottom teeth while you breathe out. Pushing the tongue firmly against your teeth when taking the slow and controlled breathe actually opens up the parasympathetic side of your nervous system and can relax your body very quickly.
- Use mediation CDs.

Progressive muscle relaxation

This technique allows you to identify areas of muscle tension and reduce that tension through simple muscle movements. Many people are tense without knowing it. They have held their muscles tight for so long that it feels normal to them. In this way they experience stress.

The following exercise will help you recognise more easily when your muscles are tense and when they are relaxed. Once you can do this you can learn to release the tension quickly and easily before it troubles you. You can actually do 30 to 60 minutes of relaxation every day without specifically setting aside any time for this purpose.

The steps

1. Sit upright with eyes closed, palms resting on your thighs and feet flat on the floor. Proceed to tense, and then release, the muscle groups as follows. Allow sufficient time to experience the sensations fully.
2. Tighten the muscles in your feet and legs without moving the limbs.
3. Hold that tension.
4. Note how the muscles feel when they are tense.
5. Stop tensing and feel the difference.
6. Be aware of an easier, more comfortable feeling as you relax those muscles.
7. Pull in your tummy muscles but keep breathing.

- Repeat steps 1 to 4.
- Shrug your shoulders or press them down towards the floor as though lengthening your neck.
- Repeat steps 1 to 4.
- Stretch your fingers then stiffen your arms without moving them.
- Repeat steps 1 to 4.
- Clench your teeth, frown and close your eyelids tightly.
- Repeat steps 1 to 4.
- Scan your body to make sure the relaxed feelings are still there … legs … tummy … shoulders … arms … face.
- Notice the feeling of relaxation so that it becomes familiar to you and you can recapture it at will.

Chapter 17

Further Resources

A bit about eye movement desensitisation and reprocessing (EMDR)

Francine Shapiro was the founder of EMDR therapy targeting post-traumatic stress disorder (PTSD). EMDR is described as the therapy that will focus mainly on unprocessed memories and the brain. Unprocessed memories are generally trauma memories and can present as flashbacks and create emotional and behavioural reactions or symptoms that are difficult to manage. Using bilateral stimulation, rapid eye movement is simulated that allows the memory to be processed and once processed memories become less intrusive, disturbing and distressing. Treatment is generally quick especially for children and what is noticeable is the de-escalation of emotional distress, reactivity and behavioural issues.

Australian psychologists Dr Chris Lee and Dr Sarah Schubert have developed through research many EMDR protocols for working with children that present with trauma backgrounds. Dr Schubert uses EMDR for attachment work between children and carers and the results are remarkable. Definitely worth looking into for a therapeutic treatment;

check out these two websites: www.drchristopherlee.com and www.emdraa.org.

A bit about neurofeedback and biofeedback

Neurofeedback uses a kinda weird cap that is placed on the head; electrodes touch areas of your scalp that activate brainwaves. A specially designed computer game is then shown to the person while they are relaxed and calm and the person is taught how to control the game through their thoughts and ability to calm their brain. After several sessions it's hoped that the person will be able to calm themselves down by using these techniques. The American Academy of Paediatrics found that neurofeedback can successfully treat ADHD. The NSW Service for the Treatment and Rehabilitation of Torture and Trauma Survivors (STARTTS) found that neurofeedback is able to reduce anxiety and trauma symptoms in the brain such as hypervigilance and sleep issues (see https://www.startts.org.au/).

Check out the Adverse Childhood Experiences International Questionnaire (ACE-IQ). This will give you a more complex understanding of how childhood trauma impacts mental and physical health and the indicators of future social and medical issues. Also check out these websites:

- ACES Too High (www.acestoohigh.com)
- GoodTherapy (www.goodtherapy.org)
- NPR (www.npr.org)
- World Health Organization page (www.who.int)

Books

These books are a must:

- *The Body Keeps Score: Brain, Mind and Body in the Healing of Trauma* by Bessel Van der Kolk.
- *The Boy Who Was Raised as a Dog: and Other Stories from a Child Psychiatrists Notebook* by Bruce Perry and Maia Szalavitz.
- *Treating Complex Trauma in Children and their Families* by John Briere.
- *Gifts of Imperfect Parenting* by Brené Brown (all her books are fantastic).

- *The Body Remembers* by Babette Rothschild.
- *Trauma and the Body* by Pat Ogden.
- *Healing Trauma* by Dan J. Siegel.
- *Building the Bonds of Attachment: Awakening Love in Deeply Troubled Children* by Daniel A Hughes PhD (all his books are tops).
- *Affect Dysregulation and Disorders of the Self* by Allan Schore.
- *How to Stop your Words from Bumping into Someone Else's* by Sue Larkey.
- *Behaviour Solutions In and Beyond the Inclusive Classroom* by Beth Aune, Beth Burt & Peter Gennaro.
- *The Value of Play* by Perry Else.
- *Life Story Therapy: A New Therapy for Traumatised Children* by Richard Rose.

Children's books

- The *When I am feeling* series of books by Trace Moroney (fabulous books for children).
- *The Red Tree by* Shaun Tan.

Websites

- Australian Childhood Foundation (www.childhood.org.au)
- STARTTS (www.startts.org.au)
- Kidsmatter.edu.au (www.kidsmatter.edu.au)
- Ted Talks (www.ted.com)
- Australian Institute of Family Studies (https://aifs.gov.au)
- Attachment issues (check out www.danielhughes.org)

Other useful websites

- http://earlytraumagrief.anu.edu.au — for one of the best resources on isolation to connection
- www.thescienceofpsychotherapy.com — check out 'An Interview with Dr Allan Schore' (Dr Al — my hero)!
- https://www.thechaosandtheclutter.com
- www.developingchild.harvard.edu
- https://www.facs.nsw.gov.au
- https://www.adoptuskids.org/
- https://www.acu.edu.au
- https://www.afkcp.org.au
- https://www.livingwell.org.au
- http://www.fcq.com.au
- https://www.asperger.asn.au
- www.wisebrain.org
- www.kidscount.com.au
- www.earlytraumagrief.anu.edu.au
- www.ncts.net.org
- www.phoenixaustralia.org
- www.youth.anxietybc.thinkingrighttools
- https://ccyp.vic.gov.au
- www.belong-blog.com
- https://aifs.gov.au/cfca — for birth family contact, see Cathy Humphreys and Meredith Kiraly.

Glossary of Terms

Affect dysregulation	Is the inability to control or regulate emotional responses to an actual or perceived event.
Affect regulation	Is the ability to maintain a healthy level of positive feelings and manage stress reactions.
Anxiety	A feeling of worry, nervousness, distress. Can have a physical response of shakiness, sweating, racing heart, rapid breathing.
Attachment therapy	A type of psychological intervention that works with child and caregiver to increase feelings of trust, security and love.
Attention deficit hyperactivity disorder (ADHD)	Is a neurodevelopmental disorder that can be seen by persistent inattention, hyperactivity, and impulsive behaviours.
Autism spectrum disorder	Is a lifelong developmental disorder characterised by difficulties in social interaction, sensory sensitivities, difficulty with social communication and interaction and restricted or repetitive patterns of thought and behaviour. As this disorder is a spectrum disorder some people live fairly normal lives whilst others require more support with this disability.
Conduct disorder	Is a mental health disorder usually diagnosed in a child or an early adolescent that displays anti-social behaviours similar to ODD but with more vindictive, destructive and aggressive behaviours.
Dietician	An expert on nutrition and diet that is specific to the individual.
Dissociation	Occurs when the fight and flight response is not possible and our brain disconnects or separates to manage states of overwhelm. Both parts can operate independently from each other.
Empathy	The ability to understand and share feelings of another.
Flashbacks	A sudden part of a memory surfaces and causes feelings of re-experiencing the memory as if it was happening.
Hyperarousal	A state of fight or flight response with increased anxiety such as insomnia, startle responses, increased psychological and physical tension.
Hypoarousal	A freeze response, may cause emotional numbness, emptiness, sadness, irritability and low level anxiety.
Hypervigilance	State of increased anxiety with excessive vigilance, may display exaggerated feelings of being in danger or a potential threat looming.

Neurobiology	The biology of the nervous system.
Occupational therapy	The use of certain activities or tasks that help to educate or support development or recuperation from a physical, developmental, or mental illness.
Oppositional defiant disorder (ODD)	Is a childhood disorder that is described by a pattern of hostile, argumentative, disobedient and defiant behaviours.
Paediatrician	A medical practitioner/doctor specialising in children and their physical and mental health.
Reactive attachment disorder	Is a childhood disorder caused by a lack of any attachment to a caregiver from birth, this result in the child's inability to form any normal or loving relationships with others.
Reparative parenting	Parenting and providing a safe and secure environment for a child that has suffered loss in early life, therefore re-parenting the child's sense of self.
Sleep disorder	Are changes in sleep patterns such as insomnia, sleep apnoea, sleepwalking, excessive sleep and problems having uninterrupted sleep.
Strength-based approach	Focuses on the strengths of the individual or family to increase mental, emotional and physical health. Focus and increase the positives while not putting emphasis on the challenges or limitations.
Trauma-informed therapy	A three-phase approach which includes safety and stabilisation with skill development, coming to terms with traumatic memories usually through EMDR, and integration of trauma and moving on (see *Trauma and Recovery: The Aftermath of Violence* by Judith Herman).
Trigger	Is something that sets off a trauma memory or flashback making the person relive the actual event in real time.

www.ingramcontent.com/pod-product-compliance
Lightning Source LLC
Chambersburg PA
CBHW051646230426

43669CB00013B/2467